Maya Angelou's *I Know Why the Caged Bird Sings*

A CASEBOOK

CASEBOOKS IN CONTEMPORARY FICTION

General Editor, William L. Andrews

With the continued expansion of the literary canon, multicultural works of modern literary fiction have assumed an increasing importance for students and scholars of American literature. Casebooks in Contemporary Fiction assembles key documents and criticism concerning these works that have so recently become central components of the American literature curriculum. The majority of the casebooks treat fictional works; however, because the line between autobiography and fiction is often blurred in contemporary literature, a small number of casebooks will specialize in autobiographical fiction or even straight autobiography. Each casebook will reprint documents relating to the work's historical context and reception, representative critical essays, an interview with the author, and a selected bibliography. The series will provide, for the first time, an accessible forum in which readers can come to a fuller understanding of these contemporary masterpieces and the unique aspects of the American ethnic, racial, or cultural experiences that they so ably portray.

Toni Morrison's
Beloved: A Casebook
edited by William L. Andrews
and Nellie Y. McKay

Maxine Hong Kingston's
The Woman Warrior: A Casebook
edited by Sau-ling C. Wong

Maya Angelou's
I Know Why the Caged Bird Sings: A Casebook
edited by Joanne M. Braxton

Forthcoming:

Louise Erdrich's
Love Medicine: A Casebook
edited by Hertha D. Sweet Wong

MAYA ANGELOU'S

I Know Why the Caged Bird Sings

♦ ♦ ♦

A CASEBOOK

Edited by
Joanne M. Braxton

New York   Oxford

Oxford University Press

1999

Oxford University Press

Oxford   New York

Athens   Auckland   Bangkok   Bogotá   Buenos Aires   Calcutta
Cape Town   Chennai   Dar es Salaam   Delhi   Florence   Hong Kong   Istanbul
Karachi   Kuala Lumpur   Madrid   Melbourne   Mexico City   Mumbai
Nairobi   Paris   São Paulo   Singapore   Taipei   Tokyo   Toronto   Warsaw

and associated companies in
Berlin   Ibadan

Copyright © 1999 by Oxford University Press, Inc.

Published by Oxford University Press, Inc.
198 Madison Avenue, New York, New York 10016

Oxford is a registered trademark of Oxford University Press

Library of Congress Cataloging-in-Publication Data
Maya Angelou's I know why the caged bird sings :
a casebook / edited by Joanne M. Braxton.
p.   cm.—(Casebooks in contemporary fiction)
Includes bibliographical references and index.
Contents: Dolly McPherson's Initiation and discovery—Learning
to live / by Opal Moore—Reembodying the self / by Mary Vermillion—Racial
protest, identity, words and form in Caged bird / by Pierre Walker—
Maya Angelou's Caged bird / by Susan Gilbert—Death as metaphor
of self / by Liliane K. Arensberg—Singing the Black mother / by
Mary Jane Lupton—Maya Angelou, an interview with Claudia Tate.
ISBN 0-19-511606-2; ISBN 0-19-511607-0 (pbk.)
1. Angelou, Maya. I know why the caged bird sings.
2. Afro-American women authors—Biography—History and criticism.
3. Women entertainers—Biography—History and criticism.
4. Autobiography. I. Braxton, Joanne M.   II. Angelou, Maya.
I know why the caged bird sings.   III. Series.
PS3551.N464Z794   1998
818'.5409—dc21   98-13295

1 3 5 7 9 8 6 4 2

Printed in the United States of America
on acid-free paper

Credits

Maya Angelou and Joanne M. Braxton. "Interview with Maya Angelou," previously unpublished. Printed with permission of Maya Angelou and Joanne M. Braxton.

Liliane K. Arensberg. "Death as Metaphor of Self in *I Know Why the Caged Bird Sings*," originally published in *College Language Association Journal* 20, no. 2 (Dec. 1976): 273–91. Courtesy of *CLA Journal*.

Susan Gilbert. "Maya Angelou's *I Know Why the Caged Bird Sings*: Paths to Escape," originally published in *Mount Olive Review* 1, no. 1 (Spring 1987): 39–50. Courtesy of Mount Olive College Press.

Mary Jane Lupton. "Singing the Black Mother: Maya Angelou and Autobiographical Continuity," originally published in *Black American Literature Forum* 24, no. 2 (Summer 1990): 257–76. Courtesy of Mary Jane Lupton.

Dolly A. McPherson. "Initiation and Self-Discovery," originally published as Chapter 2 of *Order Out of Chaos: The Autobiographical Works of Maya Angelou* (London: Virago Press, 1991), 21–55. Courtesy of Little, Brown and Company (UK).

Opal Moore. "Learning to Live: When the Bird Breaks from the Cage," originally published in *Censored Books: Critical Viewpoints*, ed. Nicholas J. Karolides, Lee Burress, and John M. Kean (Metuchen, N.J.: Scarecrow Press, 1993), 306–16. Courtesy of Opal Moore.

Claudia Tate. "Maya Angelou," originally published as Chapter 1 of *Black Women Writers at Work* (New York: Continuum, 1983), 1–11. Courtesy of Claudia Tate.

Acknowledgments

Many people played a role in the realization of *Maya Angelou's I Know Why the Caged Bird Sings: A Casebook*. We are all indebted to Maya Angelou for her courageous life and inspiring work in the public sphere. For this book, she generously made herself available for an interview, entertained me as a guest in her home, and allowed me to attend one of her classes at Wake Forest University. I am similarly indebted to series editor William L. Andrews for his timely advice and his continuing support for my work.

During my semester as Andrew W. Mellon Professor of English at the University of Pittsburgh in Spring 1996, that department made available Alicia Fuchs, who proved an able graduate assistant.

I am indebted to the American Studies Program and the English Department of the College of William and Mary for the skills of Toby Chieffo, who transcribed the above mentioned interview, and to Casey Cornelius, Sandy Burr, and La Shonda K. Barnett, who helped with manuscript preparation. Dana Boswell, though still a graduate student in our American Studies Program, offered valuable suggestions and advice about the manuscript, some of which I accepted. Scott and Vivian Donaldson offered their warm companionship, lively conversation, and a secluded location where I could write under pressure.

Finally, I wish to thank my daughter, Mycah Brazelton-Braxton, eight years old, who has endured her mother's distractions and on some occasions, my absence. Nevertheless, my child has developed her own fascination with Maya Angelou, having written a short essay, which was posted in the hallway of her school. Mycah also presented an autographed copy of Angelou's "On the Pulse of the Morning" to the D. J. Montague Elementary School on my behalf when the scheduled assembly conflicted with my teaching responsibilities on campus. Thank you, too, Mycah, for your endless gifts, the soda can necklaces, paintings, drawings, and paper airplanes that continue both to amaze and inspire me and to lift my spirit.

Contents

Maya Angelou's *I Know Why the Caged Bird Sings*

A CASEBOOK

Symbolic Geography and Psychic Landscapes

A Conversation with Maya Angelou

JOANNE M. BRAXTON

◆　◆　◆

The ax forgets.
The tree remembers.
—Maya Angelou,
quoting an African proverb
in *Even the Stars Look Lonesome*, 1997

MAYA ANGELOU, Z. Smith Reynolds Professor of American Studies at Wake Forest University in Winston-Salem, North Carolina, is the author of five autobiographies, of which *I Know Why the Caged Bird Sings* (1970) is the first and best known.[1] Even before accepting the lifetime appointment at Wake Forest, Angelou's teaching and experience spanned not only the United States and Europe but also Africa and the Middle East.

A celebrated poet, teacher, and lecturer who has taught at the University of California, the University of Kansas, and the University of Ghana, among other places, Angelou has been honored for her academic and humanistic contributions as a Rockefeller Foundation Scholar and a Yale University Fellow. While in Ghana, she worked for the *African Review* as feature editor. Previously, while residing in Cairo, Egypt, Angelou (who speaks French, Spanish, and Fanti) edited the *Arab Observer*.

In the 1960s Angelou served as northern coordinator of the Southern Christian Leadership Conference at the invitation of Dr. Martin Luther King. She has received presidential appointments from President Gerald Ford, who asked her to serve on the U.S. Bicentennial Commission, and President Jimmy Carter, who appointed her to the National Commission on the Observance of International Women's Year. A member of the original cast of Jean Genet's *Les Blancs,* as well as the European touring company of *Porgy and Bess,* Angelou's acting credits include an Emmy Award–nominated performance as Kunte Kinte's grandmother in the televised film version of Alex Haley's *Roots.*

Without a doubt, Maya Angelou is America's most visible black woman autobiographer. While black women writers might share traditional motivations for writing autobiography, other motives derive from their unique experiences. In the eyes of the predominantly white and male culture, women, and particularly black women, speak as "others," which is to say that, at least as far as the awareness of the dominant group is concerned, the black woman speaks from a position of marginality. And yet, against all odds, she comes to self-awareness and finds herself at the center of her own experience. Veiled though she might be (even twice veiled, thrice if she should be a member of a sexual minority), the black woman autobiographer possesses her own self-conscious vision of herself and her community.[2] She sees herself and her community in relation to those who have described her as "other," and the very awareness of her enforced marginality becomes an additional catalyst for life writing, for testifying, for "telling it like it is."

Often masked, the anger of the black woman autobiographer is a deep and abiding one, as must inevitably be the case when an "othered" writer develops enough awareness of self and self-esteem to believe that her life is worth writing about. "When I pick up the pen to write," Angelou told Bill Moyers in a PBS interview, "I have to scrape it across those scars to sharpen the point."[3]

Maya Angelou has tempered her own anger and put it to a constructive purpose; her work speaks to the necessity of reflecting, remembering, opening, cleansing, healing, and, at times, issuing a warning. In *I Know Why the Caged Bird Sings,* she focuses almost entirely on the inner spaces of her emotional and personal life, crafting a "literary" autobiography that becomes not merely a personal record but also a stage on which the sins of the past can be recalled and rituals of healing and reconciliation enacted.

As I have suggested elsewhere, *Caged Bird* "is perhaps the most aesthetically satisfying autobiography written by a black woman in the years immediately following the Civil Rights era."[4] Since its initial publication almost thirty years ago, *I Know Why the Caged Bird Sings* has continually ranked on the *New York Times'* Best Seller List. *Caged Bird* has been studied by many critics; it still resonates, even with readers generations beyond its original audience. And Angelou's audience has increased along with her public

stature. The *New York Times* reported that "the week after Angelou's recitation of 'On the Pulse of the Morning' at the 1993 inauguration of President
William Jefferson Clinton, *Caged Bird*'s sales increased by nearly 500 percent,
forcing Bantam to reprint approximately 400,000 copies of the autobiography and Angelou's other works."[5]

Although *Caged Bird* has generated a substantial body of criticism and
found a solid place in the humanities curriculum, it is not a book that has
been received without controversy. According to Lyman B. Hagan, *"I Know
Why the Caged Bird Sings,* lauded by many as a literary classic which should be
read and taught to all African American young people, is one of the ten
books most frequently targeted for exclusion from high school and junior
high school libraries and classrooms."[6] Why? Poet and critic Opal Moore
puts it this way: *"Caged Bird* elicits criticism for its honest depiction of rape,
its exploration of the ugly spectre of racism in America, its recounting of
the circumstances of Angelou's own out-of-wedlock teen pregnancy, and
its humorous poking at the foibles of the institutional church.[7] Angelou
inscribes her resistance to racism, sexism, and poverty within the language,
the imagery, the very meaning of her text; her truth-telling vision confronts stereotypes old and new, revising perspective and discomforting the
reader seeking safety in the conventional platitudes of the status quo. Simultaneously, *Caged Bird*'s profoundly moral stance challenges its audience
to confront the contradictions of life and to create positive change, beginning with one's self and then one's community. As such, the task that Angelou set out for herself as a writer must be acknowledged as one of ex-
ceeding complexity; she seeks to inspire and to direct.

Angelou employs two distinct voices in *Caged Bird,* that of the mature
narrator and that of the girlchild whom Angelou calls "the Maya character" (and whom I call Marguerite). Speaking of this dichotomy, Angelou
told Claudia Tate, "I have to be so internal, and yet while writing, I have to
be apart from the story so that I don't fall into indulgence. Whenever I
speak about the books, I always think in terms of the Maya character.
. . . so as not to mean me. It's damned difficult for me to preserve this distancing. But it's very necessary."[8]

Taken together, the two voices might be seen as representing the interplay of history and memory. To borrow from the blues idiom of Ralph Ellison, the mature autobiographer consciously fingers the jagged edges of
her remembered experience, squeezing out a tough lyric of black and blue
triumph. Maya Angelou, née Marguerite Johnson, emerges miraculously
through a baptismal cataract of violence, abuse, and neglect. Evoking tran-
scendent awareness through the agency of memory, the *symbolic* Maya

Angelou rises to become a "point of consciousness" for her readers.[9] In *I Know Why the Caged Bird Sings*, the reader might hear echoes of Gorky or Dostoyevsky, Zora Neale Hurston or Richard Wright, yet Angelou signifies on these inherited models to "sing" her sassy song of the self.

Among the many possible approaches to the writing of an introduction to this collection of essays on *I Know Why the Caged Bird Sings*, I opt for an exploration of the ways in which Maya Angelou's autobiographical voice embodies memory. Critics of fiction and nonfiction alike agree that memory is a "plastic" medium through which the past can be seen and reconstructed. "[M]emory is almost sacred," wrote French historian Pierre Nora.[10] And Melvin Dixon saw memory as a tool that could be used both to dismantle and reclaim. In his words, "Memory becomes a tool to regain and reconstruct not just the past but history itself."[11] Putting it another way, critic and writer Karen Fields wrote, "[M]emory collaborates with forces separate from actual past events, such as an individual's wishes, a moment's connotations, an environment's clues, an emotion's demands, a self's evolution, a mind's manufacture of order, and yes, even a researcher's demands."[12] Toi Derricotte expressed it simply and more elegantly, perhaps, when she wrote, "Memory is in the service of the greatest psychic need."[13]

The collection is framed by two interviews and begins here in the introduction (as it ends in Claudia Tate's well-known piece from *Black Women Writers at Work*) with Angelou's own words. In the fall of 1996, I visited Angelou at her home in Winston-Salem, North Carolina, having obtained permission to interview her for this book. That interview is embodied within the text of this introduction. Fascinated by the theoretical interplay between history and memory (and what Melvin Dixon called "strategies of recollection"), I asked Angelou about her writing technique and, specifically, how she uses memory to "reenter" historical time.

JOANNE BRAXTON: If you think now about the actual historical moment and what was going on in your mind when you were a child and then when you think of what memory has done to that moment, does the memory seem very different?

MAYA ANGELOU: What I remember I remember completely. Whole scenes play themselves against roads and farmland. I can remember the aroma in the air, the background sounds. . . . On the other hand, if I don't try to remember it, then whole things are lost completely. It has been that way with me all of my life.

So what happens when I write autobiographies is that I try to suspend myself from the present. I get myself into a time, into a particular day and I'm there. Each time that I do that, I am also aware that I might not come out, that I might be trapped in that time—it's frightening.

I keep a hotel room and I go to it about five thirty in the morning and pull off my coat. I have a yellow pad and the Bible. I get on the bed and try to find that entry. It is so scary. It is so physical that by twelve o'clock I'm just wet. Soaked. Then I get up and take a shower at the hotel and go home. Sometimes I will cook, make a pot of soup, say, and then go back to the hotel again and write.

BRAXTON: How does it feel to sit there holding that tattered old paperback copy of *I Know Why the Caged Bird Sings* with this nearly thirty-years-younger Maya Angelou on the cover?

ANGELOU: It's like seeing a movie, one that's known, maybe one that's written. It's not painless to remember.

BRAXTON: The life is not painless . . . the remembered life? Or the writing?

ANGELOU: All of them! I just turned to (putting down the book) something I haven't thought about in a long time. When my father . . . see, so many things come to mind. . . . I mean, I was very kind in this remembrance . . . When I left my father's house, or the house that he took me to . . . he came back to give me a dollar and a half.

I grew up that day terribly.

If Angelou here admits employing a self-censoring "strategy of recollection," this selective remembering might be an example of what Karen Fields calls the "'wedding list' or 'church program' sort of memory." Often this sort of memory, with its emphasis on "the utter necessity of getting it right," as Fields points out, does not like to be questioned or verified.[14]

During our conversation, Angelou spoke at length about shattering experiences of racism, sexism, and poverty represented in *Caged Bird*—experiences viewed through the lens of memory. To aid in exploring the relationships among history, memory, and writerly craft in *Caged Bird,* I asked Angelou to diagram the yard, the house, and the immediate environs of the Wm. Johnson General Merchandise Store in Stamps, Arkansas (generally known as Sister Henderson's Store).

Within this cleanly swept yard, ten-year-old Marguerite experiences what she describes in *Caged Bird* as the "most painful experience that I ever had with my grandmother." In this confrontation, Mrs. Annie Henderson, Marguerite's grandmother and her absolute protector, positions herself as a literal barrier between her family and a "dangerous" white world, even though she must subject herself to racial insult to do so. Even when verbally assaulted by the adolescent girls, Momma Henderson remains outwardly "cool," giving no visible sign of her inner turmoil. During our interview, Angelou explores perspectives she withheld when writing this critical scene in *Caged Bird.*

BRAXTON: Let's talk about the geography, the physical geography of your grandmother's yard. Please draw or diagram things in your grandmother's yard? Could you situate the store . . . would you mind?

ANGELOU: O.K. There is the store. Out the back door . . . that's the back door . . . out the back door as you come out and to the left there is a garden—this is the garden—and behind the garden there is a chicken coop right there. And over on the right as you came out of the back door, there were two ways out of the back of the house . . . this was the bedroom. . . .

Over here was the pigs' sty as you turn right. This is the kitchen, which was about here; out that door were steps, and this was my uncle's bedroom with Bailey, and my grandmother's bedroom with me was here. And here was the kitchen; all the rest of this was store. There was a window here, near my grandmother's bedroom, and then a window here, and there was a big door to the store; this was the front door.

Here, outside, was the real living area. This was a chinaberry tree. My grandmother had a table built around the chinaberry tree so people could sit there under it. On Saturdays, women would come there and get their hair done and ladies would come, hairdressers. Men would barber around this chinaberry tree. At one point, we had lawn here, where we could play croquet, in the back, because in front of the house was dirt. I raked the dirt . . . here from the front porch back to the chinaberry. There were wash pots, right here, huge wash pots, and over there was a well where we drew water.

BRAXTON: Pots for washing clothing?

ANGELOU: Um hum, big iron pots. We boiled clothes in one and one was for rinsing, and there was a clothesline from that tree [to] another tree. The road came right across here and so there was a drive, I mean, for people who had cars or wagons.

Along here, this was the way to town, and this was the way to Mrs.

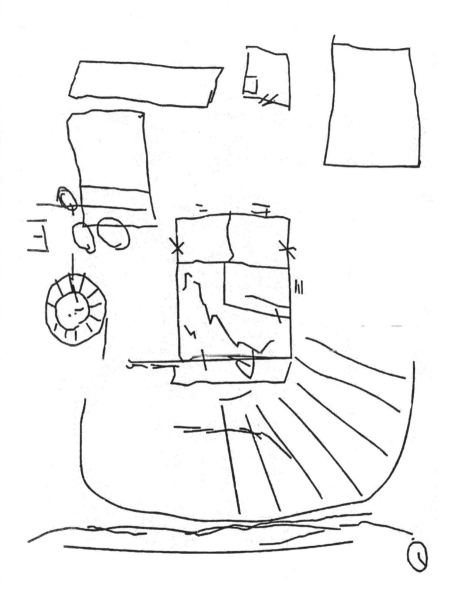

Drawing of Maya Angelou's backyard.

Flowers' house. The school was still up here, up the hill. So, you could see from the porch—well, you could just see the path, there wasn't a road, but a path up to the school.

The toilet was between the pigs' sty and the chicken coop. And there was a door, and over here there was a box, and in the box there were all sorts of interesting things like Sears and Roebuck catalog pages used for [toilet] paper, but also nice magazines like *Liberty* and *Good Housekeeping*, *Ladies' Home Journal*, and one of those little Christian things that Momma thought should go out there and wouldn't be sacrilegious to put out in the toilet. They were never used—these [Christian] magazines—for paper, only the Sears Roebuck catalog.

Now the [white] girls came along this road, and they'd walk in front of the house, in front of the store. Whenever Momma or anybody saw white girls coming, they'd call Uncle Willie and tell him to hide. Because these girls, or women, for that matter, could come in the store and say, "I'll have two pounds of this . . . I'll have ten pounds of this . . . I'll have so and so." And then they would say, "Put it on my bill, Willie." And my uncle could not say, "You don't have a bill," because all they would have to do is say, "He tried to touch me."

They knew they couldn't blackmail Grandmother. There was no point coming into the store and getting candy or trying to. They showed out because my grandmother was so impregnable. She was a fortress that could not be entered into.

BRAXTON: Are you saying that there is a sexual dynamic in the backdrop of this exchange even though everyone who is involved in chapter five is female?

ANGELOU: Absolutely.

BRAXTON: There is an implied threat to your Uncle Willie?

ANGELOU: That's right, and to my brother, Bailey. ALWAYS a threat.

The white and female "children" deliberately exploit their protected status to intimidate and humiliate Mrs. Henderson and her family. Despite the almost ritual insult by the three taunting girls, Mrs. Henderson remains, in symbolic memory and as represented in the text of *Caged Bird*, nearly impassive. Only her apron strings flutter as the girls flaunt their imagined racial superiority.

What is the source of the narrator's selective remembering here? Is the version represented by the narrator in *Caged Bird* a sanitized example of "wedding list" or "church program" memory? Is the mature autobiographer's decision based on aesthetics? Or was Angelou, when writing, aware that a radically different treatment of this scene of confrontation, one that took into account all of its racial and sexual implications, might cause her book to be viewed as "just another protest work," possibly limiting her audience? If so, did her strategy of recollection collaborate with that awareness? I probed further.

BRAXTON: During the exchange in the yard, the "Maya character" reflected that there was a shotgun loaded and tucked away. Did she have any awareness of what it would have meant to use that gun?

ANGELOU: The four hundred and ten. My Uncle Willie always called it the four hundred and ten. . . .

I knew that killing was a sin. I knew that you weren't supposed to do anything to whites, not speak to them or even look them in the eye. I also knew that whites could and did do anything to us.

At my grandmother's quilting bee, five or six of her lady friends would quilt, and they had a big rack and they'd put it in her bedroom, which was really part living room too. They rolled out the quilt, and the ladies would do that fine stitching. And they would talk, and if I could keep really quiet just outside the door I could overhear them.

The women would tell the most stories about black men being lynched, black men running away, white men they worked for trying to get to them, and white women pretending they didn't see it, didn't see the husband try to feel them up. White women being angry with the black woman for even being an object of sexual desire to their husbands, not ever angry with the husband. So I heard all of that, and I knew, had to know, have some inkling of, lots of things. Of course, I didn't understand all of the implications, but you couldn't be black in the South past five years of age and not know the threats implied and overt.

BRAXTON: In *I Know Why the Caged Bird Sings,* you write about many terrible experiences. How did you emerge from the chrysalis of Maya's vulnerability? What enabled you to heal yourself where another person might have been destroyed? What was the difference?

ANGELOU: I can't remember a time when I wasn't loved by somebody. So even in the bad, really bad times, in Saint Louis, my brother, Bailey, helped. When I couldn't really trust my mother or her mother, or my uncles . . . they amused me, of course . . . they were funny . . . but to trust them?????

My grandmother loved me and Uncle Willie loved me UNCONDI-
TIONALLY . . . even when I became so weird that they couldn't understand me—they loved me. They loved me even then. . . .

And my grandmother to my knowledge never once kissed me, but
she'd stroke my hair and pat me and say, "Poor girl." That was the equiva-
lent to sitting in her lap, you know. Momma would look at my hair and
say—and I would sit on the floor—and she would say, "Momma will plait
your hair."

She'd cook for me. Whatever she cooked was everybody's dinner, but
she would say, "Marguerite, you've got bumps on your face and I'm gonna
make you some greens." Now that was everybody else's dinner too, but
I knew it was for me and whatever bumps I had had to leave, and
they would. That knowledge in itself is a healing lard, an ointment, a
lotion. It is true therapy, true. And sometimes, I mean in the crisis, in the
maelstrom, one may not think about the fact that one is loved. But you
come out of that maelstrom, you come through the storm because of it.
You see?

That's what I mean by love. I don't mean indulgence. The larger society
could say anything it wanted, anything about me, but my grandmother
said I was somebody.

BRAXTON: I'm sure that you knew that you would be criticized for writing
about the rape. Why did you do it?

ANGELOU: Writing is very hard for me. Writing well, that is, telling the
truth, is almost impossible. Anything I write, I write because I have to
write. And I have to tell the truth about it, not just facts about it. If I could
get away with it, inside myself, I would write the facts. But if I start to
write, I have to write the truth.

The rape of a child is the cruelest action because it has so many implications. The child is, herself, himself, the potential rapist. Many people who
have been raped quite often go to violate everything: themselves first, and
then their families, their lovers, then the community and the society. It is
so awful. I can say, honestly, that I don't believe a day has passed that I
haven't thought about it, in something I do, in my own sexuality, in my
own practices. So I thought to myself, "You write so that perhaps people
who hadn't raped anybody yet might be discouraged, people who had
might be informed, people who have not been raped might understand
something, and people who have been raped might forgive themselves."

That's why I wrote about the rape.

Everything costs, Joanne Braxton, everything costs, everything, all the time. I am always amazed to see photographs of myself. I always look like I'm about to cry, and I have reason for it.

The essays that follow, all previously published, provide a range of perspectives on *I Know Why the Caged Bird Sings* and offer appropriate contextualization and a variety of critical approaches that support sound readings of the text not only by scholars of autobiography and black and women's studies but also by a more general audience reading Angelou's work for pleasure. Dolly McPherson's "Initiation and Self-Discovery" is placed first because it establishes a literary and cultural context, examining the ways in which *Caged Bird* forever reconfigured African-American autobiographical expression and paved the way for future generations of black women writers. McPherson theorizes about the autobiographer's use of memory to recreate herself in the light of her own method and the ways in which the amazing popularity of *I Know Why the Caged Bird Sings* over a period of thirty years parallels Angelou's emergence as a public figure. In McPherson's words, "[C]ritics had no reason to think that a first book by an entertainment personality would be of particular importance. . . . For Angelou, however, the autobiographical mode was to become the means to an enduring public career."[15] This is a worthwhile observation, for even in the United States, a country that has emerged or "grown up" with the autobiographical genre, the writing of literary autobiography has rarely been a route to such popular acclaim.

Opal Moore's "Learning to Live: When the Bird Breaks from the Cage" originally appeared in a volume on censorship. With First Amendment rights under fire from religious conservatives, and *Caged Bird* one of the most frequently banned books in American schools, no discussion of this book can be complete without a consideration of the problem of censorship. Moore asks the critical question, "Will children be harmed by the truth?" She argues that *Caged Bird,* at once so race- and gender-specific and at the same time universal, "transcends its author." *Caged Bird* must not be banned, Moore says: "[A] younger audience . . . needs to know that their lives are not inherited or predestined, [and] that they can be participants in an exuberant struggle to subjugate traditions of ignorance and fear." Indeed, Moore lauds *Caged Bird* as "a book that has the potential to liberate the reader into life," a viewpoint shared by many parents, teachers, and critics.[16]

Mary Vermillion writes about somatophobia, or fear of the body, specifically fear of the black female body in this case, in *I Know Why the Caged Bird Sings.* Vermillion's essay "Reembodying the Self: Representations of Rape in *Incidents in the Life of a Slave Girl* and *I Know Why the Caged Bird Sings"* examines issues of rape, voice, and literary empowerment. According to Vermillion, "The woman who records her own rape must—if she does not wish to do with her pen what Lucrece does with her sword—close the distance between her body and whatever her society posits as a woman's integral self (i.e., sexual reputation, mind, soul, desire, or will)."[17]

Vermillion explores a fear and disdain for the body that decidedly fosters the oppression of black women in somatophobic societies. The prevalence of somatophobia complicates wildly the task of the African-American woman who would remember publicly her own rape. Vermillion asserts that the black woman writer "must recover and celebrate her body without reinforcing racist perceptions of her as mere body."[18] Moreover, she argues that *Caged Bird* continues in the tradition of Harriet Jacobs's *Incidents in the Life of a Slave Girl* by challenging and subverting the somatophobia inherent in patriarchal societies that posit blacks and women as being more bodylike, more sensual.

Pierre A. Walker writes about *Caged Bird* as "literary autobiography," focusing on form. In his "Racial Protest, Identity, Words, and Form," Walker proposes the "difficulty of writing autobiography 'as literature.'" Analyzing Angelou's seamless narrative and "the formal ways *Caged Bird* expresses its points about identity, words, and race," Walker comments on the "internal organization of chapters" and their thematic juxtaposition. Walker demonstrates that in *Caged Bird,* "the political and the formal [are] . . . inextricably related" both to each other and to the development of Angelou's aesthetics.[19]

In "Paths to Escape," Susan Gilbert examines the two voices of *Caged Bird,* "the child, growing to consciousness of herself and the limits of her world, and the author, experienced, confident, and didactic."[20] Unlike the hero of the *bildungsroman,* Marguerite, the lonely and isolated heroine of *Caged Bird,* like many others in the black female autobiographical tradition, narrates a collective story wherein she transcends loneliness and pain and ultimately finds her way to survival, fulfillment, and the realization of a self-defining identity.

Liliane K. Arensberg's "Death as Metaphor of Self" traces Angelou's "protean and existential" movement, and her continual "reorientation and assimilation" as defining themes of her identity. Arensberg also examines Angelou's ambivalent feelings about her mother, including fear, love, desire, and rage. Facing the very real threat of violence from potential white lynchers, Marguerite Johnson balances her fear with a "revenge fantasy" in which "Gabriel Prosser and Nat Turner had killed all whitefolks in their beds and . . . Abraham Lincoln had been assassinated before the signing of the Emancipation Proclamation, . . . Harriet Tubman had been killed by that blow on her head and Christopher Columbus had drowned in the *Santa Maria*" (*Caged Bird,* 152–53).[21] This fantasy reshapes history through public remembering in service of a deep need to overcome the weight of the past, a past in which black folks and Indians, viewed in a more conventional historical light, always lose out.

In "Singing the Black Mother: Maya Angelou and Autobiographical Continuity," Mary Jane Lupton argues that Maya Angelou's autobiographical series is, "like an unfinished painting," an "ongoing creation, in a form that rejects the finality of a restricting frame." "What distinguishes . . . Angelou's autobiographical method," Lupton argues, "is her very denial of closure. . . . Angelou, by continuing her narrative, denies the form and its history, creating from each ending a new beginning, relocating the center to some luminous place in a volume yet to be."[22] Lupton argues that, at this point, there can be no closure to Angelou's continuing narrative. A careful look at the body of Angelou's oeuvre confirms Lupton's argument. The volumes of Angelou's autobiographical writing that follow, *Gather Together in My Name* (1974), *Singin' and Swingin' and Gettin' Merry Like Christmas* (1976), *The Heart of a Woman* (1981), *All God's Children Need Traveling Shoes* (1986), and her essays and poetry, many of which have autobiographical content, suggest a fluidity of form and a layered or accretive approach to self-representation that transcends any narrow definition of genre.[23]

In closing, Claudia Tate's classic interview from *Black Women Writers at Work* discusses, among other things, Angelou's philosophy on the importance of image making, especially for black women writers. Angelou speaks very consciously about her role as an image maker, especially as young black postmodernists seek responsible mentors after whom they may model useful and responsible lives. And the casebook ends, as it began, with Angelou's own words.

Thirty years ago Maya Angelou was a virtually unknown black entertainment figure and a survivor of poverty, abandonment, child abuse, and unwed motherhood. Autobiography, beginning with the publication of *Caged Bird* in 1970, is at least partially the answer to the phenomenon of Angelou's unprecedented ascent to the podium where she would read "On the Pulse of the Morning" to celebrate the inauguration of an American president, the first black and the first woman ever honored to be commissioned to write a public poem for such an occasion.

Who is the "phenomenal woman" known as Maya Angelou (née Marguerite Johnson)? "Dr. Angelou" to her students and colleagues at Wake

Forest University, "Dr. A." to her staff, "Sister" to her colleague and friend Professor Dolly McPherson, "Aunty" to her niece Rosa Johnson, and "Grandmother" to her beloved grandson Colin Ashanti Murphy Johnson. Like the little girl Marguerite whom she has somehow kept alive within her memory and her spirit all of these years, Angelou has continued to grow, returning continually to the black experience for models and inspiration.

While Angelou has overcome much through personal courage, humor and romance, love and laughter have played important roles in her continuing quest for growth and renewal. As I was about to conclude our interview in Winston-Salem, I asked an open question, which, characteristically, she used to teach me about the importance of something I had overlooked—in this case, romance.

BRAXTON: Is there anything that I didn't ask you that I should have asked you?

ANGELOU: Yes, you should have asked me about romance!

BRAXTON: What about romance?

ANGELOU: That's a good question! [Laughter] I think it is very important in everybody's life. Without romance we risk being brutish and bland. Without romance we might have our sexual needs satisfied, but just that . . . just that. I think that black women tend to be romantic much longer than white women, so that in my late sixties I find myself as sexually excited as I was in my late forties, for that matter, and excitable.

I have to tell you a story about my mom. My mom was married to Poppa and Poppa was my stepfather, but he had never had any children. So, I was his first child as far as he was concerned, his first daughter. He probably had been about sixty-nine. He and my mother married when my mother was sixty-nine. They have been together for a few years, but they married on her sixty-ninth birthday. So, when she was about seventy-four, she called me from Scotland, California, where she lives and she said, "Baby, I'm through with your daddy. I'm through with him, I mean it— you better talk to him."

So I said, "What is it Mom?"

"Well you see, he thinks just because he had a stroke, that sex is dangerous for his heart," she said. "I told him, what better way to die?" She said, "and he thinks I can be satisfied with just having sex once a month . . . I'll put his butt out on the street, you better talk to him."

I said, "Mom, I don't know how . . ."

She said, "You're the only one who can."

I said, "O.K., you leave the house at 5:30. You go somewhere at 5:30 this afternoon." I thought all day, I prayed, and finally I called him, six o'clock, their time. I said, "Hey, Pop."

And he said, "Baby, how you doing down there in North Carolina."

I said, "Pretty good, Poppa. Let me speak to Mother."

He said, "She's out. She went over to your cousin Katie's."

I said, "Oh, she's not feeling very well is she?"

He said, "Yeah, she's feeling really good . . ."

I said, "Poppa, she is not eating."

And he said, "Yes she is."

I said, "You mean she's got an appetite?"

He said, "Sure, your momma's got an appetite."

I said, "She's not cooking."

He said, "Yes she is, she made that wonderful lunch for me today and we had it together . . . she's got a good appetite."

I said, "But she's not drinking."

He said, "Yes she is, she had . . ."

"Yeah, but Poppa I'm trying to get a picture of her, cause I see her as losing her appetite."

He said, "No, no she's got a good appetite."

I said, "Listening to music?"

He said, "Listening to Take Six this morning. We put it on that sound system you gave her."

I said, "But she's not playing those cards . . ."

He said, "She is over at your cousin Katie's right now; you know they playing those bones."

"So what you are saying, Poppa, is that all of her appetites are good?"

He said, "Yes ma'am, I can tell you that."

I said, "Poppa listen, please excuse me, but all of her appetites are good, but you see that means that she has got only one appetite that you can satisfy and . . ." I said, "Poppa please . . . Poppa, I have to tell you that she has gone needing in some area that only you can . . . Poppa please excuse me, the fact is she's desperate Poppa . . ."

He said, "Goodbye."

I hung up the phone.

The NEXT morning, my mother calls: "Hello, Mother's Little Diamond!"

Full of the joys and sorrows of the real world in all of their complexity, Maya Angelou offers her readers the possibility that they might experience the fullness of their own lives and be baptized into an awareness of the mystery and wonder of what it means to live and breathe and love and walk this earth of terrible and terrifying beauty. Hers is a road map that cries out for each reader to reinvent herself—in short, to become her own mother.

Notes

1. Angelou's other four autobiographies are *Gather Together in My Name* (1974), *Singin' and Swingin' and Gettin' Merry Like Christmas* (1976), *The Heart of a Woman* (1981), *All God's Children Need Traveling Shoes* (1986).

2. In the introduction to *Black Women Writing Autobiography: A Tradition Within a Tradition* (Philadelphia: Temple University Press, 1989), I revise DuBois's definition to argue that there are gender-specific veils of perception, language, reference, and allusion within the veil of blackness. See pages 1–8.

3. Maya Angelou, speaking to Bill Moyers, "Creativity with Bill Moyers," PBS Video, CEL Communications, Inc., 1981.

4. Braxton, *Black Women Writing Autobiography,* 13, 181–82.

5. Nadine Brozan, "Chronicle," *New York Times* (late/final edition), January 30, 1993.

6. Lyman B. Hagan, *Heart of a Woman, Mind of a Writer, and Soul of a Poet* (Lanham, Md.: University Press of America, 1997), 148–49.

7. Opal Moore, "Learning to Live: When the Bird Breaks from the Cage" in *Censored Books: Critical Viewpoints,* ed. Nicholas J. Karolides, Lee Burress, and John M. Kean (Metuchen, N.J.: Scarecrow Press, 1993), 306–07.

8. Claudia Tate, "Maya Angelou," in *Black Women Writers at Work* (New York: Continuum, 1983), 3.

9. In "Richard Wright's Blues," from *Shadow and Act* (1953, 1964), Ralph Ellison wrote, "The blues is an impulse to keep the painful details and episodes of a brutal experience alive in one's aching consciousness, to finger its jagged grain, and to transcend it, not by the consolation of philosophy but by squeezing from it a near-tragic, near-comic lyricism." (See Ralph Ellison, *Shadow and Act* [New York: Harper and Row, 1953, 1964], 78.)

James H. Cone calls the blues "secular spirituals," because while they "confine their attention solely to the immediate and affirm the bodily expression of the black soul . . . ," they have theological significance in the sense that they are "impelled by the same search for the truth of the black experience" as the spiritual. (See James H. Cone, *The Spirituals and the Blues: An Interpretation* [Maryknoll, N.Y.: Orbis

Books, 1997], 100.) Like the preacher or the blues singer, Angelou assumes a representative and symbolic role, speaking for others who might remain largely voiceless while investing certain authority in the annointed representative.

10. Pierre Nora, as quoted by Melvin Dixon, "The Black Writer's Use of Memory" in *History and Memory in African American Culture,* ed. Genevieve Fabre and Robert O'Meally (New York: Oxford University Press, 1994), 18.

11. Melvin Dixon, in *History and Memory,* 18–19.

12. Karen Fields, "What One Cannot Remember Mistakenly," in *History and Memory,* 150.

13. Toi Derricotte, *The Black Notebooks* (New York: Norton, 1997), author's preface.

14. Fields, 152.

15. Dolly McPherson, *Order Out of Chaos: The Autobiographical Works of Maya Angelou* (London: Virago Press, 1991), 23 and 22.

16. Moore, 306, 308, and 314.

17. Mary Vermillion, "Reembodying the Self: Representations of Rape in *Incidents in the Life of a Slave Girl* and *I Know Why the Caged Bird Sings," Biography: An International Quarterly* 15, no. 3 (Summer 1992): 244.

18. Ibid., 245.

19. Pierre A. Walker, "Racial Protest, Identity, Words, and Form in Maya Angelou's *I Know Why the Caged Bird Sings," College Literature* 22, no. 3 (Oct. 1995): 91, 105, 99, and 94.

20. Susan Gilbert, "Maya Angelou's *I Know Why the Caged Bird Sings:* Paths to Escape," *Mount Olive Review* 1, no. 1 (Spring 1987): 39.

21. Liliane K. Arensberg, "Death as a Metaphor of Self in *I Know Why the Caged Bird Sings," College Language Association Journal* 20, no. 2 (Dec. 1976): 277 and 283.

22. Mary Jane Lupton, "Singing the Black Mother: Maya Angelou and Autobiographical Continuity," *Black American Literature Forum* 24, no. 2 (Summer 1990): 257 and 258.

23. In a brief introduction to the reprint of Nellie Arnold Plummer's *Out of the Depths: Or the Triumph of the Cross,* I discuss the discontinuous narrative form employed by some African-American autobiographers and compare it to the construction of the memory jar, a monument honoring a deceased loved one. The memory jar has some of the qualities of a quilt or "comforter" made from familiar material and scraps of worn-out clothing. It too "comforts," but the quilt is pieced together, while the memory jar is layered, with objects embedded in the plaster surface sometimes overlapping. (See Braxton, introduction, *Out of the Depths: Or the Triumph of the Cross* [New York: G. K. Hall, 1997].)

Like the multiple surfaces overlaying the brown glass of the memory jar, Angelou's five narratives build one upon the other, occasionally overlapping the poetry and autobiographical essays. For the writer, one of the unique advantages of the "layered" form of the accretive narrative is that it allows many voices to speak and more than one story to be told. Accretive forms occur naturally in the folk discourse of oral cultures; if one speaker lays down the thread of a well-known narrative, another might pick it up. In Angelou's larger narrative, the emerging Mayas carry the story, engaging in a call and response both with the imagined reader and earlier selves, sometimes within the same text. Through this process, the Maya-myth emerges.

Initiation and Self-Discovery

DOLLY A. MCPHERSON

◆ ◆ ◆

> We are a tongued folk. A race of singers. Our lips
> shape words and rhythms which elevate our spirits
> and quicken our blood. . . . I have spent over
> fifty years listening to my people.
> —Maya Angelou

> I think of my life and the lives of everyone who has
> ever lived, or will ever live, as not just journeys
> through time but as sacred journeys.
> —Frederick Buechner,
> *The Sacred Journey*

> The longest journey is the journey inwards.
> —Dag Hammarskjöld, *Markings*

UNTIL MAYA ANGELOU published the first volume of her autobiography, no one could have predicted that she would achieve such
popular recognition, as distinct from the esteem that many black writers,
such as Sterling Brown, Langston Hughes, Gwendolyn Brooks, Robert
Hayden, and Margaret Walker, had long enjoyed in academic and literary
circles. *I Know Why the Caged Bird Sings,* published in 1970, broke ground in
terms of critical acclaim, and large sales throughout the country presaged
the success soon afterward of such writers as Rosa Guy, Louise Merri-
wether, Verta Mae Grosvenor, and Alice Walker.

Maya Angelou started writing relatively late in life and was forty-one
when *I Know Why the Caged Bird Sings* (hereafter called *Caged Bird*) was published. Her adult life up to then had been a dizzying succession of mini-
careers, many of which are described in the five volumes of the autobiography. For Angelou, however, the autobiographical mode was to become the

means to an enduring public career. Written at the urging of friends who were overwhelmed and fascinated by the stories she told about her childhood, her grandmother in Arkansas, and her mother in California, Angelou recalls that she was "roped" into writing this first volume:

> At the time, I was really only concerned with poetry, though I had written a television series. James Baldwin took me to a party at Jules and Judy Feiffer's home. We enjoyed each other immensely and sat up until three or four o'clock in the morning drinking scotch and telling tales. The next morning Judy Feiffer called a friend of hers at Random House and said, "You know the poet Maya Angelou? If you can get her to write a book. . . ." When Robert Loomis, Judy's friend and an editor at Random House called, I told him that I was not interested. Then I went to California to produce a series for WNET. Loomis called me two or three times, but I continued to say that I was not interested. Then, I am sure, he talked to Baldwin because he used a ploy which I am not proud to say I haven't gained control of yet. He called and said, "Miss Angelou, it's been nice talking to you. But I'm rather glad that you decided not to write an autobiography because to write an autobiography as literature is a most difficult task." I said, "Then I'll do it." Now that's an area I don't have control of yet at this age. The minute someone says I can't, all of my energy goes up and I say, "Yes, I can." I believe all things are possible for a human being, and I don't think there is anything in the world I can't do.[1]

On February 12, 1970, the date on which *Caged Bird* was launched publicly, critics had no reason to think that a first book by an entertainment personality would be of particular importance, although on that day the book received a noteworthy review in the *New York Times.* Shortly thereafter, in the March 2, 1970, edition of *Newsweek,* critic Robert A. Gross praised *Caged Bird,* noting that it "was more than a tour de force of language or the story of childhood suffering because it quietly and gracefully portrays and pays tribute to the courage, dignity and endurance of the small, rural Southern Black community in which [Angelou] spent most of her early years in the 1930's."[2] At about the same time, Edmund Fuller observed in his *Wall Street Journal* review that "only the early signs of artistry and intellectual range are in this story, but their fulfillment are as evident in the writing as in the accomplishments of Maya Angelou's varied career."[3] Before the end of the year, other critics were heralding *Caged Bird* as marking the beginning of a new era in the consciousness of black men and women and creating a distinctive place in black autobiographical tradition.

Caged Bird is a carefully conceived record of a young girl's slow and clumsy growth. It is also a record of her initiation into her world and her discovery of her interior identity. In *Caged Bird,* Angelou first confidently reaches back in memory to pull out the painful times: when she and her brother Bailey fail to understand the adult code and, therefore, break laws they know nothing of; when they swing easily from hysterical laughter to desperate loneliness, from a hunger for heroes to the voluntary pleasure-pain game of wondering who their *real* parents are and how long it will be before they come to take them to their *real* home. Growing up in Stamps, Arkansas, as Maya Angelou describes those long-ago years, is a continual struggle against surrender to the very large adults, who, being black, practiced and taught special traditions whose roots were buried in Africa or had been created during centuries of slavery. According to these traditions, a good child dropped her eyes when speaking to an adult; a good child spoke softly; a good child never resisted the idea that whites were better, cleaner, or more intelligent than blacks. Growing up and surviving as a young girl in the South of the 1930s and early 1940s is a painful experience for a young girl whose world is colored by disillusion and despair, aloneness, self-doubt, and a diminished sense of self.

Indeed, Angelou underscores her diminished sense of self and the rootlessness of her early childhood years when she proclaims in the prologue:

> "What are you looking at me for?
> I didn't come to stay. . . ."[4]

The words are painfully appropriate, for the young Maya, then Marguerite Johnson, is a shy, tensely self-conscious child who believes that her true beauty is obscured. As she struggles to remember her lines, she is conscious of her dual self, which is the constant subject of her fantasies. Beneath the ugly disguise—a lavender taffeta dress remade from a white woman's discard, broad feet, and gap-teeth—is the real Marguerite.

Such fantasies are ephemeral, and the time comes when the young girl must face the painful reality of her being. Angelou recalls that

> Easter's early morning sun had shown the dress to be a plain ugly cut-down from a white woman's once-was-purple throwaway. It was old-lady-long too, but it didn't hide my skinny legs, which had been greased with Blue Seal Vaseline and powdered with Arkansas red clay. The age-faded color made my skin look dirty like mud, and everyone in church was looking at my skinny legs.[5]

For Maya there is no magical metamorphosis, no respite from her "black dream." On this Easter Sunday, she understands the futility of her wish to become "one of the sweet little white girls who were everybody's dream of what is right with the world."[6] Unlike Christ, whose resurrection from death the church is commemorating, Maya cannot be reborn into another life where she will be white and perfect and wonderful.[7] Pained by this reality and by the impossibility of her white fantasy, Maya flees from the church "peeing and crying" her way home.

This scene re-creates graphically the dynamics of many young black girls' disillusionment and imprisonment in American society. In *Black Rage,* psychiatrists William H. Grier and Price M. Cobb describe this "imprisonment":

> If the society says that to be attractive is to be white, [the black woman] finds herself unwittingly striving to be something she cannot possibly be; and if femininity is rooted in feeling oneself eminently lovable, then a society which views her as unattractive and repellent has also denied her this fundamental wellspring of femininity.[8]

The young Maya not only lives in a society that defines beauty in white terms of physical beauty, but she also internalizes these notions. In a letter (February 4, 1966) to her longtime friend Rosa Guy, Angelou wrote, "My belief [as a child] that I was ugly was absolute, and nobody tried to disabuse me—not even Momma. Momma's love enfolded me like an umbrella but at no time did she try to dissuade me of my belief that I was an ugly child."[9]

In this letter and in the autobiography as well, Angelou offers important insights into the effects of social conditioning on the mind and emotions of a black child growing up in a hostile environment. Writing from the perspective of adulthood, the older Angelou reveals that, within this imprisoning environment, there is no place for the young Maya, that she is a displaced person whose pain is intensified by her awareness of her displacement.[10] "If growing up is painful for the Southern Black girl, being aware of her displacement is the rust on the razor that threatens the throat. It is an unnecessary insult."[11] Such truths characterize important segments of Angelou's life and provide wide-ranging, significant themes for the work.

Yet Angelou does not relate all facets of her childhood experiences. Rather, through a series of episodic chapters, she selects and chronicles those incidents from which she, as a girlchild, learned valuable, life-determining truths about the world, about her community, and about herself—truths incarnated in moments of insight (initiation) and discovery of self. By identifying these epiphanies, the reader is able to define the unique vision of the work and its precise and individual illumination of reality.

After the prologue, the reader meets two children, ages three and four, who are wearing wrist tags that identify them as Marguerite and Bailey Johnson, Jr. A note addressed "To Whom It May Concern" states that they are traveling alone from Long Beach, California, to Stamps, Arkansas, to the care of Mrs. Annie Henderson. Angelou explains that she and her brother Bailey were shipped to the home of their paternal grandmother when their parents decided to end their calamitous marriage. The porter, who was charged with their welfare, ends his assignment the next day in Arizona, but before leaving the train he pins their tickets to Bailey's inside coat pocket. From that day until the day of their arrival in Stamps, the children are literally on their own. This episode further defines the dynamics underlying Angelou's battered self-esteem. Early on, when the young Maya fantasizes that she is white, blond, and beautiful, she does so because, in reality, she sees herself as a child whom no one could possibly love, certainly not her mother or father, who have so totally rejected her.

Maya and Bailey reach safely their destination and gradually adjust to their new life in Stamps, becoming integral parts of Grandmother Henderson's store and religion, of Uncle Willie's life, and of the community itself, a community that closes around the children "as a real mother embraces a stranger's child. Warmly but not too familiarly."[12]

There are nights when Maya and Bailey cry and share their loneliness as unwanted children who have been abandoned by their divorced parents. They also share their questions: Why did they send us away? What did we do so wrong? Why, at three and four, did we have tags put on our arms to be sent by train alone from Long Beach, California, to Stamps, Arkansas, with only the porter to look after us?[13] Unable to accept the fact that they have been abandoned, Maya and Bailey convince themselves that their mother is dead because they cannot bear the thought that she "would laugh and eat oranges in the sunshine without her children."[14] Comforted by the imagined reality of her mother's death, Angelou, recalling the child's emotional response, writes:

> I could cry anytime I wanted to by picturing my mother (I didn't know what she looked like) lying in her coffin. Her hair, which was black, was spread out on a tiny little pillow and her body was covered by a sheet. The face was brown, like a big O, and since I couldn't fill in the features I printed MOTHER across the O, and tears would fall down my cheeks like warm milk.[15]

Angelou recalls vividly the assault to the young Maya's diminished sense of self when she receives her mother's first Christmas presents. The tea set and a doll with blue eyes, rosy cheeks, and yellow hair are all symbols of a white world foreign to the child's experience. Not only is her mother alive, as the presents prove, but Maya, the five-year-old herself, has been the forgotten child during her two years of separation from her mother. The young Maya may, in time, be able to forgive her mother, but for the moment she must face the unimaginable reality of being both unwanted and abandoned.

Even if Angelou had focused on only the psychological trauma of her early years or had merely probed the fragile relationship between the environment and her coming-of-age, *Caged Bird* would merit the critical acclaim it has received. Clearly, the autobiography does much more. While Angelou constantly demonstrates the "unnecessary insult" of Southern black girlhood in her passage from childhood to adolescence, at the same time she skillfully re-creates those psychic, intellectual, and emotional patterns that identify her individual consciousness and experience. In doing so, the autobiographer gives concrete embodiment to such significant themes as death, regeneration, and rebirth and thus makes a creative and imaginative use of the Christian myth.

Angelou's childhood is molded by her wise, hard-working grandmother, Mrs. Annie Henderson, in a community where weekly church services, periodic revival meetings, and occasional confrontations with whites punctuate the young girl's education. A tough-minded businesswoman who purchased her store and first parcel of land in 1910 with $1,000 in dimes earned from her sale of meat pies and lemonade, Grandmother Henderson is not demonstrative in her love for Maya. Yet she is uncompromising in that love. A model of righteous behavior and a source of knowledge and pride, she sustains the young Maya during one of the most difficult periods of her life. Moreover, she gives the child the kind of nurturing that will later fortify her to face her growing-up years and the outside world. From a childhood still vivid in her mind, Angelou recalls that "a deep-brooding love hung over everything she touched."[16]

Through this indomitable woman, Maya is introduced to the spiritual side of black life. Portrayed as an individual whose world is ordered by work, duty, "her place," and religion, Grandmother Henderson represents the religious tradition begun in secret praise meetings during slavery and further developed in the small frame churches that once dotted the countryside and small American towns. Much of the strength of the black woman in general and of Grandmother Henderson in particular can be attributed to the black church. From slavery to emancipation, blacks found solace in the biblical injunction to "refrain thy voice from weeping, and thine eyes from tears: for thy work shall be rewarded" (Jeremiah 31:16). A strongly devout woman, Grandmother Henderson begins each morning with a traditional prayer of thanks and supplication, one often heard in black American churches through individual witness and testimony:

> Our Father, thank you for letting me see this New Day. Thank you that you didn't allow the bed I lay on last night to be my cooling board, nor my blanket my winding sheet. Guide my feet this day along the straight and narrow, and help me to put a bridle on my tongue. Bless this house and everybody in it. Thank you, in the name of Your Son, Jesus Christ, Amen.[17]

To Grandmother Henderson, God is a real and personal friend. In the spirit of many black Americans of her time, her understanding of Biblical teachings has persuaded her that blacks are God's chosen vessels, that He will punish those who torment His people. As God protected the Jews from Pharoah, she believes that God, in His own time and in His own way, will protect and deliver blacks. Until that day comes, she teaches Maya and Bailey to rely on the promises of a just God, to avoid contact with whites where possible, and to follow the paths of life that she and her generation had found to be safe ones. She also teaches them to respect piety and those customary laws that governed all areas of a "good" child's life and behavior. According to this rigid code, cleanliness is next to Godliness, dirtiness the inventor of misery. An impudent child is not only detested by God and a shame to its parents, but will also bring destruction to its house and life. Through the purity of her life and the quality of her discipline, Mrs. Annie Henderson demonstrates that, by centering one's being in God, one can endure and mitigate the effects of an unjust world. Angelou internalizes these silent lessons. Indeed, she owes much of her clarity of vision to her grandmother, who though not always able to protect herself and family from the exterior climate of hate, refuses to diminish herself as a human being by succumbing to bitterness or by engaging in aggressive, retaliatory behavior. Like any caring adult who has been charged with the responsibility of rearing a child, Mrs. Henderson knows that she must not only interpret society to Maya but also equip her with the pertinent skills and attitudes that will allow her to survive. While she is often unrelenting in her punishment (i.e., when she gives Maya a severe beating for using the expression "by the way") and has little time or inclination to verbalize affection, Mrs. Henderson does manage to usher Maya safely through her childhood and early adolescence.

Angelou recalls that in Stamps "segregation was so complete that most Black children didn't really, absolutely know what Whites looked like."[18]

Yet the white world remained an ever-hovering, dreaded threat. Total awareness of this threat led to a clearly defined pattern of behavior on the part of blacks and respect for certain codes of conduct if one was to survive in the South. One respected, though unwritten, law was "The less [one said] to Whitefolks (or to even powhitetrash) the better." Moreover, as Angelou writes, Momma "didn't cotton to the idea that Whitefolk could be talked to at all without risking one's life." [19]

Angelou's consciousness of the oppression suffered by black Americans is honed by the realities of Maya's daily experience, the most difficult of which force her to acknowledge that like Grandmother Henderson, Uncle Willie, and Bailey—like all those she knows to be good and worthy—she is also bound to be affected by forces outside her control or comprehension.

Angelou recalls a painfully confusing incident that occurred when she was ten years old, an incident that she later would judge to be a pivotal experience in her initiation because it taught her an important lesson about her grandmother's ability to survive and triumph in a hostile environment. The incident involves three young white girls who are known to nettle blacks and who have come onto Grandmother Henderson's property to taunt the older black woman with their rudeness, to ape her posture and mannerisms, and to address her insolently by her first name. Throughout this scene, she stands solidly on her porch, smiling and humming a hymn. When their actions produce no results, the girls turn to other means of mockery, making faces at Mrs. Henderson, whispering obscenities, and doing handstands. The young Maya, who observes this painful scene from inside the store and suffers humiliation for her grandmother, wants to confront the girls directly, but she realizes that she is "as clearly imprisoned behind the scene as the actors outside [are] confined to their roles." [20]

Throughout the incident, Mrs. Henderson is a pillar of strength and dignity, standing tall and firm. As the girls take leave, they yell out in succession, "Bye, Annie." Never turning her head to acknowledge their departure or unfolding her arms, she responds, "Bye, Miz Helen, 'bye Miz Ruth, 'bye Miz Eloise." [21] Enraged by her grandmother's seeming subservience and powerlessness, Maya cries bitterly. Later, however, when she looks up into the face of her grandmother, who is quietly standing over her, she sees her face as "a brown moon that [shines] on [her]." Angelou recalls this moment:

> She was beautiful. Something had happened out there, which I couldn't completely understand, but I could see that she was happy. Then she bent

down and touched me as mothers of the church lay hands on the sick and afflicted—and I quieted.

"Go wash you face, Sister." And she went behind the candy counter and hummed, "Glory, glory, hallelujah, when I lay my burden down."

I threw well water on my face and used the weekday handkerchief to blow my nose. Whatever the contest had been out front, I knew Momma had won.[22]

This scene is a dramatic, symbolic re-creation of the kind of spiritual death and regeneration Angelou experienced during the shaping of her development. But it is also a vivid recapturing of black/white tensions in the South of the 1930s. On the one hand, three white girls, attempting to use their race as an overbearing instrument of power, treat a black woman like another child, practicing the rituals of white power with the full sanction of the white community and attempting to reduce the black woman to their level. On the other hand, the black woman chooses the dignified course of silent endurance. Although Mrs. Henderson knows that she must accord the girls some modicum of respect, she refuses to recognize them as anything but white children, refuses to register their offensiveness or humanity, refuses to play their game. Seeking to preserve her own integrity and to transcend the ugliness of their actions, Mrs. Henderson wins a psychological victory by using this weapon to transcend the limitations of her social world.[23]

White dominance intrudes on other occasions that also teach Maya vital lessons in courage and survival and open her eyes to the fact that she belongs to an oppressed class. In Uncle Willie, for example, she sees the dual peril of being black and crippled when he is forced to hide in the potato bin when the sheriff casually warns Grandmother Henderson that local white lynchers will be on a rampage in the black community. Through this terrifying experience, Maya learns that lameness offers no protection from the wrath of bigots.

Other occasions provide proof of a predatory white world and of white ritualistic violence against the black male—for example, when Bailey sees the castrated body of a black man. Horrified by what he has seen but not understood, Bailey begins to ask questions that are dangerous for a young black boy in the Arkansas of 1940. The incident leads Angelou to conclude bitterly that "the Black woman in the South who raises sons, grandsons and nephews had her heartstrings tied to a hanging noose."[24] Years later, when Angelou must fight for the opportunity to become the first black person hired as a conductor on the San Francisco streetcars, she learns that

white racism is not merely a problem of the South but an evil that pene-
trates most aspects of American life.

While intrusion from the outside world provides experiences that in-
crease the child's awareness of her social displacement, the Store, where
blacks congregate before and after work, teaches Maya the meaning of economic discrimination. By keenly observing the cotton workers who visit
the Store, she gains insight into their inner lives. In the early dawn hours,
Maya observes the cotton workers, gay and full of morning vigor, as they
wait for the wagons to come and take them to the fields. Optimistic that
the harvest will be good and not choosing to recall the disappointments
of the recent past, the workers josh each other and flaunt their readiness
to pick two or three hundred pounds of cotton this day. Even the children
promise "to bring home fo' bits."[25] The later afternoons, however, reveal
the actual harshness of black Southern life. In the receding sunlight, "the
people [drag themselves], rather than their empty sacks."[26] Angelou writes:

> Brought back to the Store, the pickers would step out of the backs of trucks
> and fold down, dirt-disappointed, to the ground. No matter how much
> they had picked, it wasn't enough. Their wages wouldn't even get them out
> of debt to my grandmother, not to mention the staggering bill that waited
> on them at the white commissary downtown.
>
> The sound of the new morning had been replaced with grumbling
> about cheating houses, skimpy cotton and dusty rows. In later years I was to
> confront the stereotyped picture of gay song-singing cotton pickers with
> such inordinate rage that I was told even by fellow Blacks that my paranoia
> was embarrassing. But I had seen the fingers cut by the mean little cotton
> bolls, and I had witnessed the backs and shoulders and arms and legs resist-
> ing any further demand.[27]

In cotton-picking time, the late afternoons reveal the harshness of black
Southern life, which in the early morning had been softened by nature's
blessing of grogginess, forgetfulness, and the soft lamplight.

While *Caged Bird* vividly protrays the negative social and economic texture of Stamps, Arkansas, Maya Angelou, like many other black autobiographers, describes the Southern black community as one that nurtures its
members and helps them to survive in such an antagonistic environment.
There are numerous examples that demonstate the communal character
of life in Stamps. People help each other. During the Depression when no
one has money, Grandmother Henderson employs a system of barter to
help her neighbors and thus to save her store. When the wife of an old
friend dies and the widower is unable to accept his loss, Grandmother

Henderson and Uncle Willie, without a moment's hesitation, invite him to share their home, although space is limited and the guest will have to sleep on a pallet in Uncle Willie's small bedroom. When Bailey does not return from a movie at his usual time, the black men and women share Grandmother Henderson's concern. One member's concern becomes the community's concern because members, in their practice of the rituals of extended family relationships, are related not only through the community but through the church as well.

Innumerable passages in *Caged Bird* provide a sense of the black community, a sense of oneness, a sense of fused strength. The changing seasons, for example, provide opportunities for fellowship and festivity. In winter, after the first frost, hog killings are spirited events that demonstrate community linkages and strength. Everyone is an important participant in this annual rite. As Angelou describes it,

> The missionary ladies of the Christian Methodist Episcopal Church helped Momma prepare the pork for sausage. They squeezed their fat arms elbow deep in the ground meat, mixed it with gray nose-opening sage, pepper and salt, and made tasty little samples for all obedient children who brought wood for the slick black stove. Then men chopped off the larger pieces of meat and laid them in the smoke-house to begin the curing process. They opened the knuckle of the hams with their deadly-looking knives, took out a certain round harmless bone ("it could make the meat go bad") and rubbed salt, coarse brown salt that looked like find gravel, into the flesh and the blood popped to the surface.[28]

In a very direct way, the church-related activity also speaks to the particularly American value of self-reliance, a value that is necessary for survival in a hostile social world. Unlike the white American, in order for the individual black American to be self-reliant, he or she must rely on the community.[29]

Angelou's generalized description of a summer picnic fish fry conveys the vigorous solidarity of the entire black community. Everyone is there: church groups, social groups (Elks, Eastern Stars, Masons, Knights of Columbus, Daughters of Pythias), teachers, farmers, field-workers. Free from their daily chores, excited children run about in wild play, and "the sounds of tag beat through the trees."[30]

Musicians perform, displaying their artistry with "cigar-box guitars, harmonicas, juice harps, combs wrapped in tissue papers, and even bathtub basses."[31] The harmony of a gospel group "float[s] over the music of the country singers and melt[s] into the songs of small children's ring games."[32] The amount and variety of food further underscore the importance of the event. The autobiographer recalls:

> Pans of fried chicken, covered with dishtowels, sat under benches next to a mountain of potato salad crammed with hard-boiled eggs. . . . Homemade pickles and chow-chow, and baked country hams, aromatic with cloves and pineapples, vied for prominence. . . . On the barbecue pit, chickens and spareribs sputtered. . . . Orange sponge cakes and dark brown mounds dripping Hershey's chocolate stood layer to layer with ice-white coconuts and light brown caramels. Pound cakes sagged with their buttery weight. . . . And busy women in starched aprons salted and rolled . . . fish in corn meal, then dropped them in Dutch ovens trembling with boiling fat.[33]

Through such lyrical reminiscences of childhood, Angelou celebrated the richness and warmth of Southern black life, as well as the bonds of community, with all of its possibilities for love and laughter that often persist in the face of poverty and oppression. In Maya Angelou's vision, both with respect to the black community and to herself, what is kept consistently in focus is the attempt to preserve and celebrate humanity in the face of seemingly impossible odds. *Caged Bird* testifies to the amazing resilience of black Americans and their ability to cope with the inequities of American racism. The first volume of her autobiography bears witness to the sense of relationships in the black community—the cooperative alliances that enable blacks to survive, with grace and exuberance, the most difficult circumstances. For the young Maya, the black community is the essential community.

When Maya is seven years old, she sees her parents for the first time in her memory. Bailey, Sr., making an unexpected visit to Stamps, stuns the child by the reality of his presence. For the first time in her young life, she need create no elaborate fantasies about her father. Bailey, Sr., who has been described by others as a man who has respect for neither morals nor money,[34] is an arrogant show-off, taller than anyone Maya has ever seen and with "the air of a man who [does] not believe what he [hears] or what he himself is [saying]."[35] Yet Maya is fascinated by his ironic pretentiousness. In her fantasy world, her father lives richly, among orange groves and servants in the kind of elegantly furnished mansions she has seen in the movies. In time, however, Maya learns that he is merely a doorman at the Breakers Hotel in Santa Monica, California. She also learns that her father's real purpose in coming to Stamps is to deliver her and Bailey to their mother in St. Louis. Maya is terrified by the thought of seeing her elusive mother. She wants to beg her grandmother to allow her to remain in Stamps, even if she must promise to do Bailey's chores and her own as well, but she does not have the nerve to try life without Bailey, who is overjoyed by the prospect of joining his "mother dear." The day finally arrives when Maya, bidding a tearful farewell to Grandmother Henderson and Uncle Willie, must leave Stamps behind. A few days after the uneventful trip to St. Louis, Bailey, Sr., returns to California. Maya is neither glad nor sorry when this stranger leaves.

If Bailey, Sr., represents some distant world unknown to Maya, Vivian Baxter's world is equally foreign. Vivian Baxter, Maya's lively, beautiful mother, is bold, self-reliant, and unconventional. Although a trained surgical nurse, she does not work at her profession because neither the operating room nor the rigid eight-to-five schedule provides the excitement she craves. Rather, she cares for herself and children through liaisons with a variety of live-in "boyfriends" who furnish the necessities and through the extra money she earns cutting poker games in gambling parlors. Men are permitted to remain with Vivian Baxter only as long as they follow her strict code of conduct; one has been cut and another shot for failing to show proper respect for her prerogatives.

For Maya, Stamps and St. Louis stand in sharp contrast. In Stamps, there are Grandmother Henderson and the Store; there are also religious devotion and the acceptance of one's worldly and racial lot. In the closely knit rural community, Maya knows all the black people in town, and they know her. For the young Maya, Stamps is a symbol of order; in fact, the orderliness of the Store—the carefully arranged shelves, the counters, and the cutting boards—reflects the orderliness of her life in general. In St. Louis, however, Angelou is thrown into her mother's world of taverns, pool halls, gambling, fast living, and fast loving. This is a far looser environment than Maya has ever known and one that is devoid of the customary laws that Grandmother Henderson had taught her to respect. The range of sanctioned behavior is also broader; individuals are less stringently controlled by moral laws or social pressures; and relations among individuals are less stable. Although Maya lives comfortably in St. Louis and is excited by many aspects of urban life, she remains a stranger among strangers, mainly because the urban community treats the individual as individual rather than as part of a group, and so is powerless to provide her the emotional security she needs.[36] Moreover, having spent four years in the solitude of Stamps, Maya is dislocated by the strangeness of her new environment: the tremendous noise of the city, its "scurrying sounds,"[37] its frightening claustrophobia. Grandmother Baxter's German accent and elegant manners are also unfamiliar. Her mother, aunts, and uncles are equally unreal. St. Louis provides Maya neither sense of place nor permanence. Indeed, after only a few weeks there, she understands that it is not her real home:

> In my mind I only stayed in St. Louis a few weeks. As quickly as I understood that I had not reached my home, I sneaked away to Robin Hood's forest and the caves of Alley Oop where all reality was unreal and even that changed every day. I carried that same shield that I had used in Stamps: "I didn't come to stay."[38]

Shifted from one temporary home to another, Maya develops a tough flexibility that is not only her protective "shield" but also her means of dealing with an uncertain world. Angelou's evocation of the palpable strangeness of the city derives from her ability, as an artist, to maintain the childlike angle of vision in re-creating this phase of her childhood.

Yet, for one brief moment, the child, deluded into a false security, fantasizes that she is at home at last with her real father. For that moment, Mr. Freeman, Vivian Baxter's boyfriend and someone whom Maya has come to love and trust, holds her close to him. Mr. Freeman's conscious violation of the child's trust, coupled with the child's own need for attention and physical closeness, leads to a further violation that the eight-year-old Maya is too young to understand:

> He held me so softly that I wished he wouldn't ever let me go. I felt at home. From the way he was holding me I knew he'd never let me go or let anything bad ever happen to me. This was probably my real father and we had found each other at last. But then he rolled leaving me in a wet place, and stood up.[39]

In the past, Maya's world had included Bailey, Grandmother Henderson, Uncle Willie, reading books, and the Store. Now, for the first time, it includes physical contact; and, while not understanding what has taken place in her mother's bed, she is anxious to repeat the experience, which has made her feel so loved and secure.

Many growing young girls, denied the emotional satisfaction of loving, concerned parents, look for emotional support at school or at play; if they are lucky, they find something that moderates their emotional discontent. Maya, however, finds little compensation of this sort. Her autobiography is singularly devoid of references to rewarding peer associations during her eight-month stay in St. Louis. She not only is dislocated by her new environment but also is alienated from any supporting peer relationships.

The second time Mr. Freeman embraces the eight-year-old girl, he rapes her. The rape, an excruciatingly painful act that involves Maya in ambiguous complicity, produces confusion, shame, and guilt. The courtroom where Mr. Freeman's trial for rape is held would be imposing to a mature, self-confident adult, but it is shattering to the child, whose confusion, shame, and guilt are further compounded by the voyeuristic aspects of the open courtroom testimony. When Maya is unable to remember what Mr. Freeman was wearing when he raped her, the lawyer suggests that she, not the defendant, is to blame for her victimization. Bewildered and frightened, Maya denies that Mr. Freeman ever touched her before the rape—partly because, in her confusion, she is convinced of her own complicity in the two sexual episodes but more because of her lifelong desire for her mother's love and approval:

> I couldn't say yes and tell them how he had loved me once for a few minutes and how he had held me close before he thought I had peed in my bed. My uncles would kill me and Grandmother Baxter would stop speaking, as she did when she was angry. And all those people in the court would stone me as they had stoned the harlot in the Bible. And Mother, who thought I was such a good girl, would be disappointed. . . .
>
>   . . . I looked at [Mr. Freeman's] heavy face trying to look as if he would have liked me to say No. I said no.
>
>   . . . The lie lumped in my throat and I couldn't get air. . . . Our lawyer brought me off the stand to my mother's arms. The fact that I had arrived at my desired destination by lies made it less appealing to me.[40]

Later, when Mr. Freeman is found murdered, Maya is convinced that he is dead because she lied—that evil flows through her mouth, waiting to destroy any person she might talk to. To protect others, she convinces herself that she must stop talking: "Just my breath, carrying my words out, might poison people and they'd curl up and die like the Black fat slugs that only pretended."[41] Acting on this conviction, Maya becomes a voluntary mute, Mr. Freeman's death having provoked not only her spiritual death but also her quasi-isolation from her world.

In Stamps, Maya could count on the unwavering support of Grandmother Henderson and the black community. However, there is a surprising inability on the part of Vivian Baxter and her family to provide adequate emotional support for Maya or to understand the psychological difficulties of an eight-year-old who has been traumatized by rape. When Maya does not behave as the person they know and accept her to be, she is punished for being so arrogant that she will not speak to her family. On other occasions, she is thrashed by any relative who feels offended by her silence. When the family can no longer tolerate Maya's "grim presence," Vivian Baxter again banishes Maya and Bailey to Stamps, Arkansas, fulfilling Maya's prophesy that she had not come to St. Louis to stay.

Maya welcomes her return to Stamps, where she finds comfort in the barrenness and solitude of a place where nothing happens. Of this Angelou writes:

> After St. Louis with its noise and activity, its trucks and buses, and loud family gatherings, I welcomed the obscure lanes and lonely bungalows set back deep in dirt yards.
>
> The resignation of its inhabitants encouraged me to relax. They showed me a contentment based on the belief that nothing more was coming to them, although a great deal more was due. Their decision to be satisfied with life's inequities was a lesson for me. Entering Stamps, I had the feeling that I was stepping over the border lines of the maps and would fall, without fear, right off the end of the world. . . .
>
> Into this cocoon I crept.[42]

In this passage and, indeed, throughout her recaptured childhood years in Stamps, Angelou examines herself introspectively. Though Angelou, the autobiographer, locates herself in the physical environment of her childhood—in a series of physical scenes—her inward retrospective musings and the interiority that she manages to capture so well are more significant to the reader's understanding of the autobiographer's private self than of the external phenomena from which the musings emerge.

Maya lives in "perfect personal silence"[43] for nearly five years until she meets Mrs. Bertha Flowers, Stamps's black intellectual, who will become for the adult Angelou her "measure of what a human being can be."[44] Mrs. Flowers throws Maya her "first life line"[45] by accepting her as an individual, not in relation to another person. Moreover, Mrs. Flowers ministers to Maya's growing hunger and quest for individuality by giving her books of poetry, talking to her philosophically about books, and encouraging her to recite poems. Committing poems to memory, pondering them, recalling them when lonely, give Maya a sense of power within herself, a transcendence over her immediate environment.

Maya's "lessons in living" with Mrs. Flowers awaken her conscience, sharpen her perspective of her environment and of the relationship between blacks and the larger society, and teach her something about the beauty and power of language. Emotionally and intellectually strengthened by this friendship, Maya begins to compose poetic verses and ring songs and to keep a scrapbook journal in which she records her reactions to and impressions of people, places, and events and new ideas that she is introduced to by books. When she is not yet nine years old, she records her impressions of early pioneer life in Arkansas:

> Such jolting, rumbling, squeaking and creaking! Such ringing of cowbells as the cattle plodded along! and dust—dust—so thick that your mouth was full of grit, your eyes were—oh, very dirty, and your hair was powdered with the reddish Arkansas dust. The sun was hot and the sweat was streaming down your face, streaking through the grime. But you were happy for you were on a great adventure. You and your father and mother, brothers and sisters, and many of your neighbors were moving from your old home in the East. You were going to settle on some rich land in Arkansas. And you were going there not on a train of railroad cars—for there were none—but in a train of covered wagons pulled by strong oxen.[46]

In this passage from Angelou's record of the historical self, one finds excellent documentation of the autobiographer's early facility with language and narrative form.

As Angelou chronicles her movements from innocence to awareness, from childhood to adolescence, there are certain social barriers that she must confront and overcome in order to maintain a sense of self and relative freedom.

For example, Angelou's first confrontation with a white person catapults her into a clearer awareness of social reality and into a growing consciousness of self-worth. This confrontation proves to be a major turning point in her life. During a brief time when she was eleven years old, Maya worked in the home of Mrs. Viola Cullinan, a wealthy, transplanted Virginian. With the arrogance of a Southern white woman whom neither custom nor tradition had taught to respect a black person, Mrs. Cullinan insults Maya by calling her Mary rather than Marguerite, a name Mrs. Cullinan considers too cumbersome. Mrs. Cullinan's attempt to change Maya's name for her own convenience echoes the larger tradition of American racism that attempts to prescribe the nature and limitations of a black person's identity. In refusing to address Maya by her proper name, the symbol of her individuality and uniqueness, Mrs. Cullinan refuses to acknowledge her humanity. A sensitive, reflective nature, combined with an alert intelligence, enables Maya to comprehend the nature of this insult. She writes:

> Every person I knew had a hellish horror of being "called out of his name."
> It was a dangerous practice to call a Negro anything that could be loosely

constructed as insulting because of the centuries of their having been called niggers, jigs, dinges, blackbirds, crows, boots, and spooks.[47]

Maya strikes back, deliberately breaking several pieces of Mrs. Cullinan's heirloom china. In doing so, she affirms her individuality and value. Through this encounter, the young Maya learns that until the individual is willing to take a decisive step toward self-definition, refusing to compromise with insults, he or she remains in a cage. In short, the individual must resist society's efforts to limit his or her aspirations. Only after Maya determines to risk Mrs. Cullinan's outrage and to defy the expectations of others is she able to begin to loose herself, psychologically, from the dehumanizing atmosphere of her environment.

Many American autobiographies besides *Caged Bird,* including *The Narrative of the Life of Frederick Douglass, Black Boy,* Maxine Hong Kingston's *Woman Warrior, The Autobiography of Malcolm X, Black Elk Speaks,* Anne Moody's *Coming of Age in Mississippi,* and others, are structured around a narrative enactment of change on two levels: the personal and psychological on one hand and the sociohistorical and intellectual on the other. Paradoxically, while Angelou is growing in confident awareness of her strength as an individual, she is also becoming increasingly more perceptive about her identity as a member of an oppressed racial group in Stamps. In Stamps, as throughout the South, religion, sports, and education functioned in ways that encouraged the discriminated class to accept the status quo. But Angelou demonstrates how blacks in Stamps subverted those institutions and used them to withstand the cruelty of the American experience.[48]

In a graphic description of a revival meeting, Angelou recalls her first observation of the relation between blacks and religion. To the casual observer, the revivalists seem to "[bask] in the righteousness of the poor and the exclusiveness of the downtrodden"[49] and to believe that "it was better to be meek and lowly, spat upon and abused for this little time"[50] on earth. Although the poor give thinks to the Lord for a life filled with the most meager essentials and a maximum amount of brute oppression, the church rituals create for them a temporary transcendence and an articulation of spirit. However, in this tightly written, emotionally charged scene, Angelou briefly records the joining point between the blues and religious traditions. Miss Grace, the good-time woman, is also conducting rituals of transcendence through her barrelhouse blues. The agony in religion and the blues is the connecting point: "A stranger to the music could not have made a distinction between the songs sung a few minutes before [in church] and those being danced to in the gay house by the railroad tracks. All asked the same questions. How long, oh God? How long?"[51]

Early on, the reader gleans that, although the Joe Louis victories in the boxing ring in the 1930s were occasions for street celebrations that caused tens of thousands of blacks to parade, sing, dance, and derive all the joy possible from these collective victories of the race, for Angelou, Joe Louis's victory over heavyweight contender Primo Carnera was "a grotesque counterpoint to the normal way of life"[52] in Arkansas. Angelou describes the scene that takes place in her grandmother's store on that night of the fight, vividly recapturing John Dunthey's style and language:

> "Louis is penetrating every block. . . . Louis sends a left to the body and it's the uppercut to the chin and the contender is dropping. He's on the canvas, ladies and gentlemen."
>
> Babies slid to the floor as women stood up and men leaned toward the radio.
>
> "Here's the referee. He's counting, One, two, three, four, five, six, seven . . . Is the contender trying to get up again?"
>
> All the men in the store shouted, "No."
>
> "—eight, nine, ten." There were a few sounds from the audience, but they seemed to be holding themselves in against tremendous pressure.
>
> "The fight is all over, ladies and gentlemen. Let's get the microphone over to the referee . . . Here he is. He's got the Brown Bomber's hand, he's holding it up . . . Here he is . . ."
>
> Then the voice, husky and familiar, came to wash over us—"The winnah, and still heavyweight champeen of the world . . . Joe Louis."
>
> Champion of the world. A Black Boy. Some Black mother's son. He was the strongest man in the world. People drank coca-colas like ambrosia and ate candy bars like Christmas. Some of the men went behind the Store and poured white lightning in their soft-drink bottles, and a few of the bigger boys followed them. Those who were not chased away came back blowing their breath in front of themselves like proud smokers.
>
> It would take an hour or more before the people would leave the Store and head for home. Those who lived too far had made arrangements to stay in town. It wouldn't do for a Black man and his family to be caught on a lonely country road on a night when Joe Louis has proved that we were the strongest people in the world.[53]

Angelou even remembers her graduation from elementary school not as the customarily exciting and happy occasion for the young graduates and their families and friends but as a dramatization of the painful injustices of a segregated society and an underscoring of the powerlessness of blacks within that society. As she listens to the insulting words of an oblivious and insensitive white speaker, the young girl perceives a terrifying truth about her racial self and about the desperation of impotence, especially about the impotence of black people in the South of the 1930s: "It was awful to be Negro and have no control over my life. It was brutal to be young and already trained to sit quietly and listen to charges brought against my color with no chance of defense. We should all be dead."[54] Yet, her momentarily mixed feelings of despair, shame, and anger on her graduation day at the seemingly hopeless future for young blacks in racist America are surmounted by her pride in blacks when the Negro National Anthem is sung. As Maya consciously joins the class and audience in singing, she unconsciously, from her perspective in time, also predicts her own future as a poet:[55]

> We survived. The depths had been icy and dark, but now a bright sun spoke to our souls. I was no longer simply a member of the proud graduating class of 1940; I was a proud member of the wonderful, beautiful Negro race.
>
> Oh, Black known and unknown poets, how often have your auctioned pains sustained us? Who will compute the only night made less lonely by your songs, or by the empty pots made less tragic by your tales?
>
> If we were a people much given to revealing secrets, we might raise monuments and sacrifice to the memories of our poets, but slavery cured us of that weakness. It may be enough, however, to have it said that we survive in exact relationship to the dedication of our poets (include preachers, musicians and blues singers).[56]

But after Grandmother Henderson and Maya are insultingly ejected from the office of a white dentist and told that he would rather stick his hand "in a dog's mouth than in a nigger's,"[57] the child can only compensate for such painful impotence by fantasizing power and triumphant revenge.

Angelou's complex awareness of what black men, women, and children encountered in their struggles for selfhood is apparent in each of these incidents. Such experiences are recorded not simply as historical events but as symbolic revelations of Angelou's inner world. They are social, geographical, and psychological occasions. The implication that one's powerlessness in the larger world may need to be experienced and overcome in the process of personal development is very clear.

In 1941, when Maya is thirteen, she and Bailey move to Oakland and later San Francisco to live with their mother, whom they have not seen in six years. By this time, Vivian Baxter has married Daddy Clidell, a gambler and respected businessman, who will soon become "the first father [Maya] would know."[58] For a while, Maya re-experiences some of the personal dis-location already felt so acutely in Stamps and St. Louis. But in time "the air of collective displacement [and] the impermanence of life in wartime"[59] dissipate her sense of not belonging. Of this she writes: "In San Francisco, for the first time I perceived myself as part of something. . . . The city became for me the idea of what I wanted to be as a grownup. Friendly but never gushing, cool but not frigid or distant, distinguished without the awful stiffness."[60]

In San Francisco, the tender-hearted girl changes into another imag-ined self: a compound of her mother, Mrs. Flowers, and Miss Kirwin of Washington High School.

Just as Stamps and St. Louis stood in sharp contrast, so do San Francisco and Stamps. From her prosperous stepfather, Maya receives a basic ghetto education:

> He owned apartment buildings and, later, pool halls, and was famous for being the rarity "a man of honor." He didn't suffer, as many "honest men" do, from the detestable righteousness that diminishes their virtue. He knew cards and men's hearts. So during the age when Mother was exposing us to certain facts of life, like personal hygiene, proper posture, table manners, good restaurants and tipping practice, Daddy Clidell taught me to play poker, blackjack, tonk and high, low, Jick, Jack and the Game. He wore ex-pensively tailored suits and a large yellow diamond stickpin. Except for the jewelry, he was a conservative dresser and carried himself with the con-scious pomp of a man of secure means.[61]

In San Francisco, Maya is also introduced to a colorful cast of urban street characters (i.e., Stonewall Jimmy, Just Black, Cool Clyde, Tight Coat, and Red Leg) who make their living through gambling and trickery. Here she learns a new morality: the black American ghetto ethic by which "that man who is offered only the crumbs from his country's table . . . by ingenuity and courage, is able to take of himself a Lucullan feast."[62] Mr. Red Leg's story, for example, is an excellent portrayal of such an individual and a brilliant recapturing of the trickster motif found in African and Afro-American literature. Through trickery, Mr. Red Leg, a con artist and a hero-figure of black American urban folklore, outwits his white antago-nist. In doing so, he symbolizes the strength, dignity, and courage black Americans are able to manifest in spite of their circumscribed lives, al-though they might function as miscreants not only in the eyes of the white world but also to the preachers and matriarchs within the black commu-nity. Black men like Mr. Red Leg, who use "their intelligence to pry open the door of rejection and [who] not only [become] wealthy but [get] some revenge in the bargain,"[63] are heroes to Maya and her "Black associates."[64]

Three other experiences further dramatize Angelou's awareness of self and her world, changing with sometimes bewildering speed, and help her to work out new patterns of selfhood and personal direction.

When she accompanies "Daddy Bailey" on a vacation to Mexico, he, having drunk quantities of tequila at a roadside bar where he has taken Maya, goes off with "his woman," leaving Maya with strangers and no money. Hours later, he returns, too drunk to drive. Rather than spending the night in the car in Mexico, Maya, who has never driven a car, manages to drive down the circuitous mountain road some fifty miles, to cross the border, and to return them safely to California. Angelou recalls:

> The challenge was exhilarating. It was me, Marguerite, against the elemental opposition. As I twisted the steering wheel and forced the accelerator to the floor, I was controlling Mexico, and might and aloneness and inexperienced youth and Bailey Johnson, Sr., and death and insecurity, and even gravity.[65]

Unlike any of her former experiences in Stamps, this single experience proves to Maya that she can indeed have power over her life and destiny.

Soon after their return to California, there is a bitter argument between Maya and Dolores (her father's current "girlfriend"), who wants Bailey's daughter out of her home and her life. Urging Maya to return to her mother, Dolores calls Vivian Baxter a whore. When Maya slaps her, Dolores cuts Maya severely. After taking her to one friend for emergency medical care, Bailey, Sr., leaves her with a second friend. Knowing that violence would ensue if she returned home and her mother learned that she had been cut, Maya leaves without telling her father or his friend and, after wandering about San Diego for some while, joins a junkyard commune of homeless children whom she describes as "the silt of war frenzy."[66] After she has spent a month in the commune, Maya's thought processes have altered so significantly that she is hardly able to recognize her former self. Her peers' unquestioning acceptance dislodges her familiar feelings of insecurity; moreover, the unrestrained life that she experiences within the group expands her spiritual horizons and "initiates [her] into the brotherhood of man."[67] The gratitude Angelou owes those who befriended her on her passage from childhood to adolescence to adulthood will forever include her junkyard family:

> After hunting down unbroken bottles and selling them with a white girl from Missouri, a Mexican girl from Los Angeles and a Black girl from Okla-

homa, I was never again to sense myself so solidly out of the pale of the human race. The lack of criticism evidenced by our ad hoc community influenced me, and set a tone of tolerance for my life.[68]

Time and time again, Angelou brings us to the question of human relationships. Through the junkyard experience, she learns that, beyond the barriers of race, all men and women are the same; they share the same fears, the same loneliness, and the same hopes. The commune experience also confirms Angelou's determination to exercise further control over her being and helps her to establish a valuable new direction for her personal growth. Months later, when Angelou becomes the first black hired as a conductor on the San Francisco streetcars, her determination and success in this venture can be directly attributed to these pivotal experiences in Mexico and California.

Angelou must confront and overcome one other obstacle before she can begin to know herself. This problem relates to numerous questions about her sexuality that plague her when she is convinced, after her third reading of *The Well of Loneliness,* that she is verging on lesbianism: Why is her voice so heavy and her hands and feet so far from being feminine and dainty? Why are her breasts so sadly underdeveloped? Is she a lesbian? Do lesbians bud gradually "or burst into being with a suddenness that dismayed them as much as it repelled society?"[69] For weeks, Angelou seeks answers to these questions, probing into unsatisfying books and into her own unstocked mind without finding a morsel of peace or understanding. When she finally approaches her mother to seek answers to the questions about her sexuality and about the disturbing physical changes that are taking place in her body, Vivian Baxter gently reassures her daughter that the physical changes are just human nature. Not altogether convinced by her mother's assurances, Maya decides that she needs a boyfriend to clarify her position to the world and to herself. From her point of view, "a boyfriend's acceptance of [her] would guide [her] into the strange and exotic lands of frills and femininity"[70] and, at the same time, confirm her heterosexuality. But among her associates, Maya cannot find an interested partner. Taking matters into her own hands, she decides to offer herself to a neighborhood youth; and, at sixteen, she becomes pregnant, a surprise consequence of a single, impersonal, unsatisfactory experiment.

Like the "aloneness" that she has experienced most of her life, Maya is literally "alone" during most of her pregnancy, for she manages to keep this fact hidden from her mother, her teachers, and her friends for eight months and one week. When Vivian Baxter learns from Maya that she will deliver a child shortly, she nurtures her daughter with understanding and support and, in doing so, becomes the compassionate, loving mother of Maya's childhood fantasies. The birth of Maya's son is a celebration of a new life, of Maya's own rebirth as a young mother, and of Maya's discovery of her creative self. But it is also an ironic outcome of a completely loveless and casual relationship.

The final scene of *Caged Bird* is richly symbolic. Maya is reluctant to let her three-week-old baby sleep with her because she is certain that she will roll over in the night and crush him. But Vivian Baxter ignores her daughter's fears and places the baby beside his mother. The next morning, Vivian Baxter is standing over her daughter. Under the tent of blanket that Maya has devised with her elbow and forearm, the baby sleeps soundly. Vivian Baxter whispers to her daughter, "See, you don't have to think about the right thing. If you are for the right thing, then you do it without thinking."[71] This scene verbalizes Vivian Baxter's faith in Maya's instinctive qualities of motherhood and Maya's acceptance of herself as a creative, life-giving force.

By the end of *Caged Bird,* the displaced young Maya has found a place and has discovered a vital dimension of herself. No longer need she ask, "What you looking at me for?" or fantasize a reality other than her own. By the end of the autobiography, Angelou, the young adult, has succeeded in freeing herself from her cage by assuming control of her life and fully accepting her womanhood. Indeed, as Sidonie Smith posits, with the birth of her child, Angelou is herself born into a mature engagement with the forces of life. In welcoming that struggle, Angelou refuses to live a death of quiet submission:[72] "Few, if any, survive their teens. Most surrender to the vague but murderous pressure of adult conformity. It becomes easier to die and avoid conflicts than to maintain a constant battle with the superior forces of maturity."[73]

Roy Pascal observes that autobiography acquires its shape through the autobiographer's consciousness of what the child ultimately became. Angelou is able to confront her memories of her own past with honesty, humor, and irony because they form a necessary part of her spiritual and intellectual development. She believes, as most autobiographers do, that memory affords access to the past that is worth revealing and that an understanding of the human condition—not information about a life, but insight into its process—is intrinsically valuable.

The narrative voice at work in *Caged Bird* is that of the older autobiographer who is not only aware of the journey but also enlarged by it, an achievement that is emphasized by the affirming nature of the work. In *Caged Bird,* Maya Angelou undergoes the archetypal American journey of initiation and discovery.

Notes

1. Maya Angelou, personal interview, Dec. 5, 1984.

2. Robert A. Gross, "Growing Up Black," *Newsweek*, Mar. 1, 1970, 90.

3. Edmund Fuller, "The Bookshelf: The Making of a Black Artist," *Wall Street Journal*, Apr. 16, 1970, 16.

4. Maya Angelou, *I Know Why the Caged Bird Sings* (New York: Random House, 1969), 3.

5. Ibid.

6. Ibid., 4.

7. Arensberg, "Death as Metaphor," 278.

8. William H. Grier and Price M. Cobbs, *Black Rage* (New York: Basic Books, 1968), 49.

9. Maya Angelou, letter to Rosa Guy, July 22, 1968, Maya Angelou Papers, Z. Smith Reynolds Library, Wake Forest University, Winston-Salem, N.C.

10. Sidonie Ann Smith, "The Song of a Caged Bird: Maya Angelou's Quest after Self-Acceptance," *Southern Humanities Review* 7 (1973): 368.

11. Angelou, *Caged Bird*, 6.

12. Ibid., 7.

13. Ibid., 51.

14. Ibid., 42.

15. Ibid., 50–51.

16. Ibid., 55.

17. Ibid., 8.

18. Ibid., 24.

19. Ibid., 46.

20. Ibid., 30.

21. Ibid., 31.

22. Ibid., 32.

23. Stephen Butterfield, *Black Autobiography in America* (Amherst: Univ. of Massachusetts Press, 1974), 211–12.

24. Angelou, *Caged Bird*, 110.

25. Ibid., 9.

26. Ibid.

27. Ibid., 9–10.

28. Ibid., 23–24.

29. See Elizabeth A. Schultz's discussion of this point in "The Insistence upon Community in the Contemporary Afro-American Novel," *College English* 41, no. 2 (Oct. 1979): 170–84.

30. Angelou, *Caged Bird*, 133.

31. Ibid., 134.

32. Ibid., 135.

33. Ibid., 134–35.

34. Dr. Lindsay Johnson, personal interview, June 16, 1983.

35. Angelou, *Caged Bird,* 53.

36. See Donald B. Gibson, "Individualism and Community in Black History and Fiction," *Black American Literature Forum* 9, no. 4 (Winter 1977): 123–29.

37. Angelou, *Caged Bird,* 68.

38. Ibid.

39. Ibid., 71.

40. Ibid., 82–83.

41. Ibid., 85.

42. Ibid., 86.

43. Ibid.

44. Ibid., 91.

45. Ibid., 92.

46. Maya Angelou, scrapbook compiled during school year 1936–37, Maya Angelou Papers, Z. Smith Reynolds Library, Wake Forest University, Winston-Salem, N.C.

47. Angelou, *Caged Bird,* 106.

48. For a fuller discussion of this idea, see Selwyn R. Cudjoe, "Maya Angelou and the Autobiographical Statement," in *Black Women Writers (1950–1980),* ed. Mari Evans (New York: Doubleday, 1984), 12–14.

49. Angelou, *Caged Bird,* 127.

50. Ibid., 128.

51. Ibid.

52. Sidonie Smith, *Where I'm Bound: Patterns of Slavery and Freedom in Black American Autobiography* (Westport, Conn.: Greenwood Press, 1974), 130.

53. Angelou, *Caged Bird,* 131–32.

54. Ibid., 176.

55. Elizabeth Schultz, "To Be Black and Blue: The Blues Genre in Black American Autobiography," *Kansas Quarterly* 7, no. 3 (1975): 88.

56. Angelou, *Caged Bird,* 179–80.

57. Ibid., 184.

58. Ibid., 203.

59. Ibid., 205.

60. Ibid., 206.

61. Ibid., 213–14.

62. Ibid., 219.

63. Ibid., 218.

64. Ibid., 219.
65. Ibid., 232.
66. Ibid., 247.
67. Ibid.
68. Ibid.
69. Ibid., 267.
70. Ibid., 272–73.
71. Ibid., 281.
72. Smith, *Where I'm Bound*, 134.
73. Angelou, *Caged Bird*, 264.

Learning to Live

When the Bird Breaks from the Cage

OPAL MOORE

◆　◆　◆

> I bring the dreaded disease. I encourage their chil-
> dren to open their hearts to the "dark" side. To
> know the fear in them. To know the rage. To know
> the repression that has lopped off their brains—
> —Toi Derricotte, "From *The Black Notebooks*"

THERE IS, IT SEEMS, a widespread movement afoot to assert the
innocence of children even as we deny or sabotage that innocence.
There is what appears to be a head-in-the-sand impulse to insist upon this
innocence by simply refusing to acknowledge its nonexistence. Never
mind the "mean streets," never mind the high teen pregnancy rates and
drug use, or the phenomenal school dropout rates, or spiraling teen suicide statistics—never mind these real dangers to childhood. There are
agencies at work to shield these unprotected children from books that
might reveal to them the workings of their own minds and hearts, books
that engender the agony of thought and the fearfulness of hope. If we
cannot protect children from experience, should we protect them from
knowing?

I Know Why the Caged Bird Sings, the autobiography of Maya Angelou, is the
story of one girl's growing up. But, like any literary masterpiece, the story
of this one black girl declaring "I can" to a color-coded society that in innumerable ways had told her "you can't, you won't" transcends its author.
It is an affirmation; it promises that life, if we have the courage to live it,
will be worth the struggle. A book of this description might seem good
reading for junior high and high school students. According to People for
the American Way, however, *Caged Bird* was the ninth "most frequently

challenged book" in American schools (Graham, 26).[1] *Caged Bird* elicits criticism for its honest depiction of rape, its exploration of the ugly spectre of racism in America, its recounting of the circumstances of Angelou's own out-of-wedlock teen pregnancy, and its humorous poking at the foibles of the institutional church. Arguments advocating that *Caged Bird* be banned from school reading lists reveal that the complainants, often parents, tend to regard any treatment of these kinds of subjects in school as inappropriate—despite the fact that the realities and issues of sexuality and violence in particular are commonplace in contemporary teenage intercourse and discourse. The children, they imply, are too innocent for such depictions; they might be harmed by the truth.

This is a curious notion—that seriousness should be banned from the classroom, while beyond the classroom the irresponsible and sensational exploitation of sexual, violent, and profane materials is as routine as the daily dose of soap opera. The degradation of feeling caused by slurs directed against persons for their race/class/sex/sexual preference is one of the more difficult hurdles of youthful rites of passage. But it's not just bad TV or the meanness of children. More and more, society is serving an unappetizing fare on a child-sized plate—television screens, T-shirt sloganeers, and weak politicians admonish children to "say 'no' to drugs and drugpushers"; to be wary of strangers; to have safe sex; to report their own or other abusing parents, relatives, or neighbors; to be wary of friends; to recognize the signs of alcoholism; to exercise self-control in the absence of parental or societal controls; even to take their Halloween candy to the hospital to be X-rayed before consumption. In response to these complications in the landscape of childhood, parent groups, religious groups, and media have called for educators to "bring morality back into the classroom" while we "get back to basics" in a pristine atmosphere of moral noncomplexity, outside of the context of the very real world that is squeezing in on that highly touted childhood innocence every single day.

Our teenagers are inundated with the discouragements of life. Ensconced in a literal world, they are shaping their life choices within the dichotomies of TV ads: Bud Light vs. "A mind is a terrible thing to waste." Life becomes a set of skewed and cynical oppositions: "good" vs. easy; yes vs. "catch me"; "right" vs. expediency.

In truth, what young readers seem most innocent of these days is not sex, murder, or profanity, but concepts of self-empowerment, faith, struggle as quest, the nobility of intellectual inquiry, survival, and the nature and complexity of moral choice. *Caged Bird* offers these seemingly abstract (adult) concepts to a younger audience that needs to know that their lives are not inherited or predestined, that they can be participants in an exuberant struggle to subjugate traditions of ignorance and fear. Critics of this book might tend to overlook or devalue the necessity of such insights for the young.

Caged Bird's critics imply an immorality in the work based on the book's images. However, it is through Angelou's vivid depictions of human spiritual triumph *set against a backdrop* of human weakness and failing that the autobiography speaks dramatically about moral choice. Angelou paints a picture of some of the negative choices: white America choosing to oppress groups of people, choosing lynch law over justice, choosing intimidation over honor. She offers, however, "deep talk" on the possibility of positive choices: choosing life over death (despite the difficulty of that life); choosing courage over safety; choosing discipline over chaos; choosing voice over silence; choosing compassion over pity, over hatred, over habit; choosing work and planning and hope over useless recrimination and slovenly despair. The book's detractors seem unwilling to admit that morality is not edict (or an innate property of innocence) but the learned capacity for judgment, and that the necessity of moral choice arises only in the presence of the soul's imperfection.

Self-empowerment, faith, struggle as quest, survival, intellectual curiosity, complexity of choice—these ideas are the underpinning of Maya Angelou's story. To explore these themes, the autobiography poses its own set of oppositions: traditional society and values vs. contemporary society and its values, silence vs. self-expression, literacy vs. the forces of oppression, the nature of generosity vs. the nature of cruelty, spirituality vs. ritual. Every episode of *Caged Bird* engages these and other ideas in Maya Angelou's portrait of a young girl's struggle against adversity—a struggle against rape: rape of the body, of the soul, of the mind, of the future, of expectation, of tenderness—toward identity and self-affirmation. If we cannot delete rape from our lives, should we delete it from a book about life?

Caged Bird opens with the poignant, halting voice of Marguerite Johnson, the young Maya Angelou, struggling for her own voice beneath the vapid doggerel of the yearly Easter pageant:

"What you lookin at me for?
"I didn't come to stay. . . ."

These two lines prefigure the entire work. "What you lookin at me for. . . " is the painful question of every black girl made self-conscious and self-doubting by a white world critical of her very existence. The claim that she "didn't come to stay" increases in irony as the entire work ultimately affirms the determination of Marguerite Johnson and, symbolically, all of the unsung survivors of the Middle Passage to do that very thing—to stay. To stay is to affirm life and the possibility of redemption. To stay—despite the circumstance of our coming (slavery), despite the efforts to remove us (lynching) or make us invisible (segregation).

Angelou, in disarmingly picturesque and humorous scenes like this opening glimpse of her girl-self forgetting her lines and wetting her pants in her earliest effort at public speech, continually reminds us that we survive the painfulness of life by the tender stabilities of family and community. As she hurries from the church trying to beat the wetness coursing down her thighs, she hears the benedictory murmurs of the old church ladies saying, "Lord bless the child" and "Praise God."

This opening recitation lays a metaphorical foundation for the autobiography and for our understanding of the trauma of rape that causes Marguerite to stifle her voice for seven years. In some ways, the rape of Marguerite provides the center and the bottom of this autobiographical statement.

Critics of the work charge that the scenes of seduction and rape are too graphically rendered:

> He [Mr. Freeman] took my hand and said, "Feel it." It was mushy and squirmy like the inside of a freshly killed chicken. Then he dragged me on top of his chest with his left arm, and his right hand was moving so fast and his heart was beating so hard that I was afraid that he would die. . . . Finally he was quiet, and then came the nice part. He held me so softly that I wished he wouldn't ever let me go. (61)

The seeming ambivalence of this portrait of the dynamics of interfamilial rape elicits distaste among those who prefer, if rape must be portrayed at all, for it to be painted with the hard edges of guilt and innocence. Yet, this portrait reflects the sensibilities of eight-year-old Marguerite Johnson—full of her barely understood longings and the vulnerability of ignorance: "Mama had drilled into my head: 'Keep your legs closed, and don't let nobody see your pocketbook'" (61).

Mrs. Baxter has given her daughter that oblique homespun wisdom designed to delay the inevitable. Such advice may forewarn but does not forearm and, characteristic of the period, does not even entertain the unthinkable improbability of the rape of a child. Aside from this vague caution and the knowledge that "lots of people did 'it' and they used their 'things' to accomplish the deed," Marguerite does not know how to understand or respond to the gentle, seemingly harmless Mr. Freeman because he is "family," he is an adult (not to be questioned), and he offers her what appears to be the tenderness she craves that had not been characteristic of her strict Southern upbringing.

When asked why she included the rape in her autobiography, Angelou has said, "I wanted people to see that the man was not totally an ogre" (*Conversations,* 156). And it is this fact that poses one of the difficulties of rape and the inability of children, intellectually unprepared, to protect themselves. If the rapists were all terrible ogres and strangers in dark alleys, it would be easier to know when to run, when to scream, when to "say no." But the devastation of rape is subtle in its horror and betrayal that creates in Marguerite feelings of complicity in her own assault. When queried by Mr. Freeman's defense attorney about whether Mr. Freeman had ever touched her on occasions before the rape, Marguerite, recalling that first encounter, realizes immediately something about the nature of language, its inflexibility, its inability to render the whole truth, and the palpable danger of being misunderstood:

> I couldn't . . . tell them how he had loved me once for a few minutes and how he had held me close before he thought I had peed in my bed. My uncles would kill me and Grandmother Baxter would stop speaking, as she often did when she was angry. And all those people in the court would stone me as they had stoned the harlot in the Bible. And Mother, who thought I was such a good girl, would be so disappointed. But most important, there was Bailey. I had kept a big secret from him. (70–71)

To protect herself, Marguerite lies: "Everyone in the court knew that the answer had to be No. Everyone except Mr. Freeman and me" (71).

Some schools that have chosen not to ban *Caged Bird* completely have compromised by deleting "those rape chapters." It should be clear, however, that this portrayal of rape is hardly titillating or "pornographic." It raises issues of trust, truth and lie, love, the naturalness of a child's craving for human contact, language and understanding, and the confusion engendered by the power disparities that necessarily exist between children and adults. High school students should be given the opportunity to gain insight into these subtleties of human relationships and entertain the "moral" questions raised by the work: should Mr. Freeman have been forgiven for his crime? (After all, he appears to be very sorry. When Marguerite awakens from the daze of trauma, Mr. Freeman is tenderly bathing her: "His hands shook" [66].) Which is the greater crime, Mr. Freeman's rape of Marguerite, or Marguerite's lying about the nature of their relationship (which might be seen as having resulted in Mr. Freeman's death)?

What should be the penalty for rape? Is the community's murderous action against Mr. Freeman's unthinkable crime merely a more expedient form of the state's statutes on capital punishment? Might we say he was "judged by a jury of his peers"? Which is the greater crime—if Marguerite had told the truth and Mr. Freeman had been acquitted, or Marguerite's lie, and Mr. Freeman's judgment by an outraged community? What *is* the truth? Didn't Marguerite actually tell the basic truth, based on her innocence, based on her inability to understand Mr. Freeman's motives? As Maya Angelou might say, "Those are questions, frightful questions, too intimate and obscenely probing" (*Black Women Writers,* 3).[2] Yet, how can we deny young readers, expected to soon embark upon their own life-altering decision making, the opportunity to engage in questions so relevant as these? How can we continue to arm them solely with T-shirt slogans?

Caged Bird, in this scene so often deleted from classroom study, opens the door for discussion about the prevalent confusion between a young person's desire for affection and sexual invitation. Certainly, this is a valuable distinction to make and one that young men and women are often unable to perceive or articulate. Angelou also reveals the manner by which an adult manipulates a child's desire for love as a thin camouflage for his own crude motives. A further complication to the neat assignment of blame is that Marguerite's lie is not prompted by a desire to harm Mr. Freeman but by her feelings of helplessness and dread. Yet, she perceives that the effect of that lie is profound—so profound that she decides to stop her own voice, both as penance for the death of Mr. Freeman and out of fear of the power of her words: "a man was dead because I had lied" (72).

This dramatization of the ambiguity of truth and the fearfulness of an Old Testament justice raises questions of justice and the desirability of truth in a world strapped in fear, misunderstanding, and the inadequacy of language. The story reveals how violence can emerge out of the innocent routines of life, how betrayal can be camouflaged with blame, and that adults are individual and multidimensional and flawed; but readers also see how Marguerite overcomes this difficult and alienating episode of her life.

However, the work's complexity is a gradual revelation. The rape must be read within the context of the entire work from the stammer of the opening scene to the elegant Mrs. Flowers who restores Marguerite's confidence in her own voice (77–87) to the book's closing affirmation of the forgiving power of love and faith. Conversely, all of these moments should be understood against the ravaging of rape.

Marguerite's story is emblematic of the historic struggle of an entire people and, by extension, any person or group of people. The autobiography moves from survival to celebration of life, and students who are permitted to witness Marguerite's suffering and ascendancy might gain in the nurturing of their own potential for compassion, optimism, and courage.

This extended look at the scene most often censored by high school administrators and most often criticized by parents should reveal that Angelou's *Caged Bird,* though easily read, is no "easy" read. This is, perhaps, part of the reason for the objections of parents who may feel that the materials are "too sophisticated" for their children. We should be careful as teachers, designers of curriculum, and concerned parents not to fall into the false opposition of good vs. easy. What is easier for a student (or for a teacher) is not necessarily good. In this vein, those parents who are satisfied to have this work removed from required lists but offered on "suggested" lists should ask themselves whether they are giving their kids the kind of advice that was so useless to Maya Angelou: "keep your legs closed and don't let nobody see your pocketbook." Without the engagement of discussion, *Caged Bird* might do what parents fear most—raise important issues while leaving the young reader no avenue to discover his or her relationship to these ideas. Perhaps the parents are satisfied to have contro versial works removed to the "suggested" list because they are convinced that their children will never read anything that is not required. If that is their hope, we have more to worry about than book lists.

If parents are concerned about anything, it should be the paucity of assigned readings in the junior high and high school classrooms and the quality of the classroom teaching approach for this (and any other) worthwhile book.[3] Educators have begun to address the importance of the preparation of teachers for the presentation of literature of the caliber of *Caged Bird,* which is a challenge not only to students but also to teachers who choose to bring this work into the classroom.[4] *Caged Bird* establishes oppositions of place and time—Stamps, Arkansas, vs. St. Louis and San Francisco; the 1930s of the book's opening vs. the slave origins of Jim Crow—that complicate images related to certain cultural aspects of African-American life. These include oral story traditions, traditional religious beliefs and practices, ideas regarding discipline and displays of affection, and other materials that bring richness and complexity to the book but, without clarification, can invite misapprehension. For example, when Marguerite smashes Mrs. Cullinan's best pieces of "china from Virginia" by "accident," the scene is informative when supported by its parallels in traditional African-American folklore, by information regarding the significance of naming in traditional society, and by the cultural significance of the slave state practice of depriving Africans of their true names and cultural past. The scene, though funny, should not be treated as mere comic relief or as a meaningless act of revenge. Mrs. Cullinan, in insisting upon "re-naming" Marguerite "Mary," is carrying forward that enslaving technique designed to subvert identity; she is testing what she believes is her prerogative as a white person—to establish *who* a black person will be, to call a black person by any name she chooses. She is "shock[ed] into recognition of [Marguerite's] personhood" *(Black Women Writers, 9)*. She learns that her name game is a very dangerous power play that carries with it a serious risk.

With sufficient grounding, *I Know Why the Caged Bird Sings* can provide the kinds of insights into American history and culture and its values, practices, beliefs, lifestyles, and seeming contradictions that inspired James Baldwin to describe the work, on its cover, as one that "liberates the reader into life simply because Maya Angelou confronts her own life with such a moving wonder, such a luminous dignity," and as "a Biblical study of life in the midst of death." A book that has the potential to liberate the reader into life is one that deserves our intelligent consideration, not rash judgments made from narrow fearfulness. Such a work will not "teach students a lesson." It will demand an energetic, participatory reading. It will demand their seriousness. With the appropriate effort, this literary experience can assist readers of any racial or economic group in meeting their own often unarticulated doubts, questions, and fears and perhaps assist in their own search for dignity.

Notes

1. Joyce Graham, in her dissertation "The Freeing of Maya Angelou's *Caged Bird,"* offers a comprehensive overview of the history of censorship efforts directed specifically against *Caged Bird*: the issues and arguments raised in connection with the teaching of the work, a look at the National Council of Teachers of English's efforts to provide guidelines for the improvement of teacher preparation in the teaching of literature, and a case study of one well-documented censorship challenge. Dr. Graham also includes an interview with Dr. Angelou discussing the nature and motive of censorship. This timely examination of the rising fear of literature in schools provides an invaluable look at the parents and administrators behind the news reports on censorship challenges.

2. Dr. Angelou makes this comment in response to her own questions: Why and how frequently does a writer write? What shimmering goals dance before the writer's eyes, desirable, seductive, but maddeningly out of reach? What happens to

the ego when one dreams of training Russian bears to dance the Watusi and is barely able to teach a friendly dog to shake hands?

3. In "The Other Crisis in American Education," college professor Daniel J. Singal discusses the decline of competency among the "highest cohort of achievers," those students who eventually apply to America's most prestigious colleges and universities. This general failing in the achievement levels of juniors and seniors is attributed to the assigning of easier, less challenging reading materials and the failure of teachers to design written and oral activities that demand higher levels of comprehension. As a result, students entering college are unable to function adequately in their coursework. Singal quotes a college professor: "No one reads for nuance. They [students] pay no attention to detail." Says Singal, "I have been amazed at how little students have managed to glean from a book I know they have read. . . . Twelve to fifteen books over a fifteen-week semester used to be the rule of thumb at selective colleges. Today it is six to eight books, and they had better be short texts, written in relatively simple English." In other words, college professors are simply unable to assign traditional work loads given the skill levels of their students.

4. Donnarae MacCann and Gloria Woodard have collected a number of essays on the images of African-Americans in literature and discussions related to children's responses to the literature. Some of the essays address the matter of censorship as it relates to racist depictions in literature. Paul Deane provides a look at the seldom-acknowledged racist images to be found in the traditional serial novels that are typically considered to be wholesome, completely unobjectionable adolescent fare.

Works Cited

Angelou, Maya. *I Know why the Caged Bird Sings* (New York: Bantam, 1969).

———. "Shades and Slashes of Light," in *Black Women Writers (1950–1980): A Critical Evaluation.* Ed. Mari Evans (Jackson, Miss.: University Press of Mississippi, 1984), 1–3.

Cudjoe, Selwyn R. "Maya Angelou and the Autobiographical Statement," in *Black Women Writers,* 6–24.

Deane, Paul C. "The Persistence of Uncle Tom: An Examination of the Image of the Negro in Children's Fiction Series" in *The Black American in Books for Children: Readings in Racism,* 2nd ed. Ed. Donnarae MacCann and Gloria Woodard. (Metuchen, N.J.: Scarecrow Press, 1985), 162–68.

Derricotte, Toi. "From *The Black Notebooks.*" *Kenyon Review* 13, no.4 (Fall 1991): 27–31.

Graham, Joyce L. "Freeing Maya Angelou's *Caged Bird.*" (Ph.D. Dissertation, Newman Library, Virginia Polytechnic Institute, Blacksburg, Va., 1991).

Singal, Daniel J. "The Other Crisis in American Education." *Atlantic Monthly* (Nov. 1991): 59–74.

Tate, Claudia. "Maya Angelou," in *Black Women Writers at Work* (New York: Continuum, 1983): 1–11. Rpt. in *Conversations with Maya Angelou.* Ed. Jeffrey M. Elliot. (Jackson, Miss.: University Press of Mississippi, 1989), 146–56.

Reembodying the Self

Representations of Rape in Incidents in the Life of a Slave Girl and I Know Why the Caged Bird Sings

MARY VERMILLION

◆　◆　◆

A STUDY OF A woman's written record of her own rape can illustrate the dual consciousness that Susan Stanford Friedman identifies as a primary characteristic of female life-writing. According to Friedman, a woman's alienation from her culturally defined self motivates the creation of an alternate self in her autobiography.[1] Because patriarchal cultural definitions of a woman center on her body and sexual status, the rape victim not only becomes painfully aware of her culturally defined self, but she also confronts a hideous paradox as she tries to construct an alternate self. In trying to perceive herself as whole and untouched, the rape victim runs the risk of fragmenting her identity, of excluding her body from what she considers as the rest of her self. Such negation of her body is a natural continuation of the actual rape: the victim tells herself that *she* was not there during the rape—it was not *she* whom he raped. Unanswerable questions then loom. If she was not there, then who was? Who is this "she," this "self" who exists bodiless?[2]

The rape victim's uncertainties about her own subjectivity stem in part from a long tradition in Western patriarchal thought—what Elizabeth Spelman terms "somatophobia," fear of and disdain for the body. Spelman demonstrates that patriarchal thinkers from Plato onward have channeled most of this disdain toward the female body.[3] I will briefly examine the partnership of misogyny and somatophobia in Shakespeare's *The Rape of Lucrece* because his poem influenced the two autobiographers whom I examine in the second and third parts of this essay. Maya Angelou specifically refers to the poem, and it shaped the novels of seduction that Harriet Jacobs critiques in her autobiography.[4] Shakespeare describes the raped Lucrece as privileging her innocent mind over her violated body: "Though my gross blood be stain'd with this abuse, / Immaculate and spotless is my mind."[5] Stephanie Jed describes how somatophobia springs from such a Platonic duality between body and mind: "Implicit in every construct of a chaste or integral mind is the splitting off of the body as the region of all potential contamination."[6] The dire but logical consequences of this splitting off emerge when Lucrece views her violated body through patriarchy's eyes. Perceiving her body as her husband's damaged property, she gives the following rationale for killing herself:

> My honor I'll bequeath unto the knife
> That wounds my body so dishonored.
> 'Tis honor to deprive dishonor'd life,
> The one will live, the other being dead.
> So of shame's ashes shall my fame be bred,
> For in my death I murther shameful scorn:
> My shame so dead, mine honor is new born.[7]

Informing Lucrece's deadly resolution are somatophobia and two other key aspects of patriarchal ideology: the identification of the female with her body and the equation of female "honor" and chastity. The destruction of Lucrece's body perpetuates these patriarchal conceptions of womanhood.[8]

The woman who records her own rape must—if she does not wish to do with her pen what Lucrece does with her sword—close the distance between her body and whatever her society posits as a woman's integral self (i.e., sexual reputation, mind, soul, desire, or will). She must reclaim her body. While this written reclamation is difficult for any woman, it presents a special problem for the black woman because of the meanings that hegemonic white cultures have assigned to her body. According to Spelman, somatophobia supports both sexist and racist thinking because these hegemonic cultures have posited women as more bodylike than men and blacks as more bodylike than whites. Within these two hierarchical relationships, the black woman is implicitly perceived as the most bodylike, and this perception fosters her oppression in somatophobic societies.[9] Numerous scholars have demonstrated that both the institutions of slavery and antebellum writing constructed the black woman as the sum total of her bodily labor and suffering. Antebellum writers—including abolitionists and black males—depicted the black woman as breeder, wet nurse, field laborer, and, most significant, sexually exploited victim. So pervasive were these images of the black woman's body that the National Association of Colored Women's Clubs, founded in 1896, targeted for its most vehement attacks negative stereotypes of black women's sexuality.[10] Angela Davis and bell hooks illustrate how these nineteenth-century stereotypes inform twentieth-century racist images of the black woman as promiscuous and bestial.[11] Because of this long history of negative stereotypes, the black woman who records her own rape faces the arduous task of reaffirming her sexual autonomy without perpetuating the racist myths that associate her with illicit sexuality. She must recover and celebrate her body without reinforcing racist perceptions of her as mere body.

This task is, of course, also a crucial project for contemporary black feminists. Reviewing Spike Lee's film, *She's Gotta Have It* (1986)—in which a black woman, Nola Darling, is raped—hooks writes:

> She [Darling] has had sex throughout the film; what she has not had is a sense of self that would enable her to be fully autonomous and sexually assertive, independent and liberated. . . . A new image, the one we have yet to see in film, is the desiring black woman who prevails, who triumphs, not desexualized, not alone, who is 'together' in every sense of the word.[12]

How two black women who have suffered rape (or its threat) begin to construct this "new image" will be my focus as I examine Harriet Jacobs's and Maya Angelou's autobiographies.

Jacobs, in *Incidents in the Life of a Slave Girl* (1861), adopts the pseudonym Linda Brent and describes how, as a young enslaved girl, she coped with the threat of rape from her master, Dr. Flint.[13] In order to escape this threat, as well as slavery itself, Brent deliberately chooses to have sexual relations with another white man, Mr. Sands. Many critics have argued that Jacobs's narration of these events echoes and subverts various components of nineteenth-century sentimental discourse—particularly the seduction plot and the basic tenets of "true womanhood" (piety, purity, submissiveness, and domesticity).[14] In my examination of these subversions, I will focus on how Jacobs critiques somatophobia and degrading images of the black female body. Brent's decision to have sexual relations with Sands marks a turning point in Jacobs's reembodying strategies. Before this point, she obscures her own corporeality in order to counter negative stereotypes about black women, and after this point, she begins constructing new positive images of the black female body.

For over one hundred years preceding Jacobs's writing of her autobiography, sentimental novelists portrayed both raped and seduced heroines as believing, like Shakespeare's Lucrece, that their sexual activities sever their integral selves from their bodies. In Susanna Rowson's *Charlotte Temple* (1791), for instance, when the eponymous heroine leaves her paternal home with her seducer, she mourns, "It seemed like the separation of soul and body."[15] Sentimental heroines who undergo such a separation (i.e., lose their "sexual purity")—be it by their own choice or not—face a bout of madness or muteness usually followed by a slow, painful death.[16] Inscribing the "fallen" woman's body as damaged male property, the sentimental novel identifies the female with her body and promotes somatophobia. Furthermore, in dishing out the same "punishment" to both raped and seduced heroines, the sentimental novel as a literary mode obscures seduction's crucial difference from rape: seduction requires a contest of wills, while rape requires the mastery of one will over another. In disguising this difference, the sentimental novel erases female volition. Jacobs, I believe, must have recognized that such an erasure reinforced the slaveholder's negation of the enslaved woman's will.[17] In order to reclaim her own volition, she appropriates the sentimental novel's obfuscation of rape and seduction. By portraying in the language of seduction her former master's legally sanctioned threat to rape her, Jacobs refutes his idea that she was his property, "subject to his will in all things."[18]

Jacobs further accentuates her own volition by depicting the unequal contest between Brent's and Flint's bodies as an equal contest of words. Observing that Jacobs's autobiography contains more reconstructed dialogue than any male-authored slave narrative, William Andrews maintains that Brent's and Flint's dialogues pivot on arguments of the slave woman's rights to define herself.[19] I want to argue that Jacobs also uses dialogue to challenge the hegemonic culture's perception of her as mere body. Flint tries to control Brent by whispering foul words into her ear, and Jacobs writes that he *"peopled* my young mind with unclean images, such as only a vile monster could think of" (27, emphasis added). With the choice of the word "peopled," Jacobs merely hints that Flint would like to "people" his plantation through Brent's body. She portrays the sexual threat that Flint poses as a predominantly psychological/spiritual one and thus lessens her reader's tendency to associate her body with illicit sexuality. Jacobs continues to mystify her former master's physical power and legal right to rape

her by confining it to verbal expressions. She primarily depicts his economic mastery over Brent not as his ability to overpower her physically
but as his power to perpetuate her slavery in his last will and testament. Jacobs further confines Flint's power to words as she portrays him sending
Brent letters, making speeches, and, ironically, promising to make her a
lady, a category from which black women were excluded by the white
planter culture.[20] Even after Brent runs away, it is Flint's words, and not his
body, that threaten her. In her first hiding place the sight of Flint gives her
a "gleam of satisfaction" (100), but the sound of his voice "chills her blood"
(103). Brent's differing reactions to Flint highlight Jacobs's primary strategy
in recording his threat to her body. As Flint's body nears Brent's, as he enters the house she hides in, Jacobs describes him as a mere voice. In recording Flint's attempts to disembody her, she disembodies him.

In thus obscuring the corporeality of Flint's threat of rape, Jacobs mini-
mizes her own body and thereby strikes a blow against the racist stereotype
of the black woman as sexually exploited victim. The pen with which she
strikes, however, is double-edged, and like Lucrece's dagger, annihilates her
own body. In the early part of her autobiography, Jacobs, like Lucrece, priv-
ileges an interior self over her body and nearly erases its presence in her text.

Brent's decision to have sexual relations with Sands, however, begins Jacobs's rewriting of her body into her life story. Most feminist readers of Jacobs's narrative interpret her discussion of this incident as her most powerful rejection of sentimental discourse and "true womanhood."[21] I want to
emphasize that Jacobs's reversals of the seduction plot's conventions also
enable her to reject the body/mind duality that promotes somatophobia.
When Flint asks if she loves the father of her unborn child, she retorts, "I
am thankful that I do not despise him" (59). Unlike the stock seduced
maiden, Brent has no uncontrollable passion for Sands. Reasoning that he
will buy and free her and the children they have, Brent exerts her own will
to escape Flint's. "It seems," she states, "less degrading to give one's self,
than to submit to compulsion. There is something akin to freedom in having a lover who has no control over you except that which he gains by
kindness and attachment" (56). Mary Helen Washington calls this declara-
tion "the clearest statement of . . . the need for control over one's female
body."[22] Jacobs, I believe, seizes this control by insisting upon a connection
between her sexuality and autonomy: "I knew what I did, and I did it with
deliberate calculation" (55). By thus emphasizing that Brent willed her
sexual activity, Jacobs critiques the somatophobic sentimental convention
that severs an unchaste woman's body from her integral self, and she inscribes Brent's union with Sands as a union of her own body and will.

After Brent escapes Flint's plantation, his pursuit of her is so rigorous that she is forced to hide for seven years in a crawl space in her grandmother's attic. Of these years in hiding Andrews writes that "her disembodied presence in patriarchal society lets her become for the first time Dr. Flint's manipulator instead of his tool."[23] While I acknowledge this power shift, I want to further explore Andrews's use of the word "disembodiment." Confined to a coffinlike space and temporarily losing the use of her limbs, Brent is indeed disembodied in her situation. Yet it is, I maintain, in describing this very disembodiment that Jacobs embodies herself in her text. Her descriptions of Brent's physical sufferings in the attic reinforce the bond between her body and her will. Jacobs engages a pattern of first cataloging Brent's physical ills and then comparing them favorably to her state as a slave:

> I was eager to look on their [her children's] faces; but there was no hole, no crack through which I could peep. This continued darkness was oppressive. It seemed horrible to sit or lie in a cramped position day after day, without one gleam of light. Yet I would have chosen this, rather than my lot as a slave. (114)

Here Brent's physical suffering accentuates not only her ability to choose but also the reason behind her choice—her children's freedom.

Jacobs also emphasizes this connection between Brent's will, body, and children by juxtaposing her agony in hiding with the pain of the slave mother whose children have been sold (122). This recurrent figure who has lost both her will and the fruit of her body represents the completely disembodied black woman. She is Jacobs's antitype and has no wish to continue her life. "Why *don't* God kill me?" asks one (16). "I've got nothing to live for now," says another (70). In chapter 13, "The Church and Slavery," Jacobs uses the disembodied slave mother to demonstrate how the somatophobic privileging of an interior self over the body disembodies the black race. In this scene not only does the childless woman voice her suffering and loss, but Jacobs also minutely records her physical torment. The woman stands and beats her breast, then sits down, "quivering in every limb." The white constable who presides over the Methodist class meeting disregards her longing for her sold children, her physical suffering, and the many enslaved people who weep in sympathy with her. He stifles a laugh and says, "Sister, pray to the Lord that every dispensation of his divine will may be sanctified to the good of your poor needy soul" (70). This "spiritual" advice disembodies the woman and her friends, leaving them only their singing voices: "Ole Satan's church is here below. / Up to God's free church I hope to go" (71). While these words disparage the white constable, they also confirm his privileging of soul over body. Critiquing the slave-holder's religion within her rewriting of the seduction plot, Jacobs juxta-poses the "Christian" slaveholder's devaluation of the black body with the sentimental novel's devaluation of the female body and thereby unveils the somatophobia in both discourses.[24]

She further contests both of these disembodying discourses with her descriptions of Brent's activities in her attic hideaway. It is in this part of the text that Brent—tearful, hysterical, and sleepless—most resembles the sentimental heroine. Brent's crawling exercises, her drilling of peep-holes, her sewing, reading, and letter writing oddly mimic domestic indus-triousness. During the second winter, in which cold stiffens her tongue, Brent's muteness and delirium echo that of a "fallen" and dying sentimen-tal heroine. Jacobs thus parallels Brent's attic with the private space that usually confines the sentimental heroine: the kitchen, the parlor, the up-stairs chamber, the deathbed, and the grave. Jane Tompkins calls such fe-male space "the closet of the heart" and observes that sentimental fiction "shares with the evangelical reform movement a theory of power that stipulates that all true action is not material, but spiritual."[25] Jacobs chal-lenges this stipulation by emphasizing the drastic material change that Brent works from within her "closet of the heart." As Valerie Smith ob-serves, Brent "uses to her advantage all the power of the voyeur."[26] She prevents her own capture by embroiling Flint in an elaborate plot to de-flect his attention, and she meets with Sands to secure his promise to free her children. In her hiding place she not only has a mystical vision of her children, but she actually succeeds in gaining their freedom from slavery.

This uniting of spiritual and material action reenacts Jacobs's earlier textual union of Brent's body and will, and it situates her maternity as a powerful symbol of her autonomy.[27] In her autobiography, Jacobs trans-forms her body from a site of sexual oppression to a source of freedom—freedom from slavery for herself and her children and freedom from so-matophobic racist ideologies that demean the black female body. With one of Brent's early experiences in the North, however, Jacobs suggests that her maternity is not the only cause for celebrating her body. Brent sees por-traits of her friend Fanny's children and remarks, "I had never seen any paintings of colored people before, and they seemed to me beautiful" (162). With this statement, Jacobs subtly indicates that her readers must likewise see the black race anew. Jacobs's autobiography, like Fanny's portraits, insists that the value and worth of the black female body exists outside of its functions in a patriarchal slaveholding society.

Important differences obviously exist between Jacobs's antebellum autobiography and Maya Angelou's twentieth-century record of her rape at age eight in *I Know Why the Caged Bird Sings* (1969). One important difference is the way in which somatophobia manifests itself in their texts. Because Angelou does not have to contend with the nineteenth-century patriarchal ideology of "true womanhood," she is freer to portray her rape, her body, and her sexuality. Yet Jacobs describes herself as beautiful and sexually desirable, while Angelou, as a child and young adult, sees herself as ugly. Jacobs posits somatophobia outside herself and critiques it as part of slaveholding culture, while Angelou portrays her younger self internalizing and finally challenging the somatophobia inherent in twentieth-century racist conceptions of the black female body. Despite these differences, Angelou's text contains reembodying strategies similar to those of Jacobs. Both women contest somatophobia by questioning religious ideologies, rewriting white literary traditions, and celebrating their bodies and motherhood as symbols of their political struggles. In order to challenge racist stereotypes that associate black women with illicit sexuality, both writers obscure their corporeality in the early part of their texts by transforming the suffering connected with rape into a metaphor for the suffering of their race. In Jacobs's text rape is a metaphor for the severed body and will of the slave, and Angelou similarly uses her rapist's violation of her body and will to explore the oppression of her black community.

Angelou first connects her rape with the suffering of the poor. "The act of rape on an eight-year-old body," she writes, "is a matter of the needle giving because the camel can't."[28] In this description, Angelou subtly links her rapist with the wealthy man whom Jesus warned would have a difficult time getting into heaven, and she reinforces this link by alluding to Jesus's words in her ironic description of a black revival congregation's sentiments: "The Lord loved the poor and hated those cast high in the world. Hadn't He Himself said it would be easier for a camel to go through the eye of a needle than for a rich man to enter heaven?" (108). As she continues to imagine the congregation's thoughts, Angelou makes the connection between her rape and the plight of the poor in class society more racially explicit, and, like Jacobs, she also demonstrates that privileging a future world over the present perpetuates black oppression:

They [the congregation] basked in the righteousness of the poor and the exclusiveness of the downtrodden. Let the whitefolks have their money and power and segregation and sarcasm and big houses and schools and lawns like carpets, and books, and mostly—mostly—let them have their whiteness. (110)

With the image of the camel and the needle, Angelou transforms her rape into a symbol of the racism and somatophobia that afflict Maya and her race throughout much of *Caged Bird.*

Rape in Angelou's text, however, primarily represents the black girl's difficulties in controlling, understanding, and respecting both her body and her words in a somatophobic society that sees "sweet little white girls" as "everybody's dream of what was right with the world" (1). Angelou connects white definitions of beauty with rape by linking Maya's rape with her first sight of her mother, Vivian Baxter. Angelou's description of Vivian echoes that of the ghostlike whites who baffle young Maya. Vivian has "even white teeth and her fresh-butter color looked see-through clean" (49). Maya and her brother, Bailey, later determine that Vivian resembles a white movie star. Angelou writes that her mother's beauty "literally assailed" Maya and twice observes that she was "struck dumb" (49–50). This assault by her mother's beauty anticipates the physical assault by Mr. Freeman, her mother's boyfriend, and Maya's muteness upon meeting her mother foreshadows her silence after the rape. With this parallel Angelou indicates that both rape and the dominant white culture's definitions of beauty disempower the black woman's body and self-expression.

Angelou further demonstrates the intimate connection between the violation of Maya's body and the devaluation of her words by depicting her self-imposed silence after Freeman's rape trial. Freeman's pleading looks in the courtroom, along with Maya's own shame, compel her to lie, and after she learns that her uncles have murdered Freeman, she believes that her courtroom lie is responsible for his death. Angelou describes the emotions that silence Maya: "I could feel the evilness flowing through my body and waiting, pent up, to rush off my tongue if I tried to open my mouth. I clamped my teeth shut, I'd hold it in. If it escaped, wouldn't it flood the world and all the innocent people?" (72). Angelou's use of flood imagery in this crucial passage enables her to link Maya's inability to control her body and her words. Throughout the text Maya's failure to keep her bodily functions "pent up" signals the domination of her body by others. The autobiography's opening scene merges her inability to control her appearance, words, and bodily functions. Wanting to look like a "sweet little

white girl," Maya is embarrassed about her own appearance and cannot remember the words of the Easter poem she recites. With her escape from
the church, Angelou implicitly associates Maya's inability to rule her bladder with her inability to speak:

> I stumbled and started to say something, or maybe to scream, but a green
> persimmon, or it could have been a lemon, caught me between the legs and
> squeezed. I tasted the sour on my tongue and felt it in the back of my
> mouth. Then before I reached the door, the sting was burning down my
> legs and into my Sunday socks. I tried to hold, to squeeze it back, to keep it
> from speeding. (3)[29]

Maya's squeezing back in this passage anticipates her stopping the flood of
her words after the rape, and Angelou also connects this opening scene of
urination with one of Freeman's means of silencing Maya. After ejaculat-
ing on a mattress, he tells her that she has wet the bed, and with this lie, he
denies her knowledge about her own body and confounds her ability to
make a coherent story out of his actions.

This inability to create a story about her body pervades the remainder
of *Caged Bird* as Maya struggles to cope with her emerging womanhood.
Angelou, however, is not content to let the mute, sexually abused,
wishing-to-be-white Maya represent the black female body in her text. Instead, she begins to reembody Maya by critiquing her admiration for white
literary discourse. An early point at which Angelou foregrounds this cri-
tique is in Maya's meeting with Mrs. Bertha Flowers. Presenting this older
black woman as the direct opposite of young Maya, Angelou stresses that
Flowers magnificently rules both her words and her body. Indeed Flowers's
bodily control seems almost supernatural: "She had the grace of control to
appear warm in the coldest weather, and on the Arkansas summer days it
seemed she had a private breeze which swirled around, cooling her" (77).
She makes Maya proud to be black, and Maya claims that Flowers is more
beautiful and "just as refined as whitefolks in movies and books" (79). Although Maya begins to respect and admire the black female body, white
heroines still provide her standard for beauty, and Angelou pokes fun at
the literary discourse that whitens Maya's view of Bertha Flowers and
womanhood:

> She [Flowers] appealed to me because she was like people I had never met
> personally. Like women in English novels who walked the moors (whatever
> they were) with their loyal dogs racing at a respectful distance. Like the
> women who sat in front of roaring fireplaces, drinking tea incessantly from

silver trays full of scones and crumpets. Women who walked over the 'heath' and read morocco-bound books. (79)

This humorous passage demonstrates that Maya's self-perception remains dangerously regulated by white culture. Angelou treats such regulation less comically when Flowers breaks Maya's self-imposed silence by asking her to read aloud. The first words Maya speaks after her long spell of muteness are those of Charles Dickens.

Angelou dramatizes the danger that a borrowed voice poses to Maya in her description of Maya's relationship with Viola Cullinan. Maya makes fun of this white woman, whose kitchen she briefly works in, until she discovers that Cullinan's husband has two daughters by a black woman. Then Maya—in a gesture of sisterhood and empathy that is never returned by Cullinan—pities her employer and decides to write a "tragic ballad" "on being white, fat, old and without children" (91). Such a ballad would, of course, completely exclude Maya's own experience: black, thin, young, and (near the end of her autobiography) with child. Through Maya's speculation that Cullinan walks around with no organs and drinks alcohol to keep herself "embalmed," Angelou implies that Maya's potential poetic identification with Cullinan nearly negates her own body. Cullinan's empty insides echo Maya's own perception of herself after the rape as a "gutless doll" she had earlier ripped to pieces (72).

Angelou's most complex and subtle examination of Maya's attachment to white literary discourse occurs when she lists as one of her accomplishments the memorization of Shakespeare's *The Rape of Lucrece*. Christine Froula maintains that Maya's feat of memory suggests the potential erasure of black female reality by white male literary discourse.[30] More specifically, I believe, Angelou's reference to *Lucrece* subtly indicates that Maya's propensity for the verbal and the literary leads her to ignore her own corporeality. After their rapes both Maya and Lucrece turn to representations of suffering women. Maya reads about Lucrece, and Lucrece, finding a painting of the fall of Troy, views Hecuba's mourning the destruction of her city and husband, King Priam. Unlike Lucrece, Maya seeks strength not from pictorial representations of female bodies but from print, and this preference for the verbal over the pictorial suggests her tendency to privilege literature over her own physical reality. Lucrece decides to speak for the mute sufferers in the painting, and Shakespeare writes, "She lends them words, and she their looks doth borrow."[31] Maya's situation is an inversion of Lucrece's lending of words and borrowing of looks. The once mute Maya can borrow Lucrece's words, but she must somehow

lend these words her own "looks" if she does not wish Shakespeare's equation of Lucrece's virtue and whiteness to degrade her own blackness.[32] In
remembering *The Rape of Lucrece* Maya must also remember or reconstruct
her own body.

One of the ways that she accomplishes this is by celebrating the bodies
of other black women. In the only story Maya creates within *Caged Bird,* she
augments her grandmother's physical and verbal powers. After a white
dentist refuses to treat Maya because she is black, Maya imagines her
grandmother ten feet tall, arms doubling in length. As this fantasy grandmother orders the dentist out of town and commands him to quit practicing dentistry, her words, too, metamorphose: "Her tongue had thinned
and the words rolled off well enunciated. Well enunciated and sharp like
little claps of thunder" (161). With Maya's brief fantasy, Angelou demonstrates how her own autobiography functions. Maya's story, which em-
powers her grandmother's body and speech, attacks the dentist's deroga-
tory behavior; Angelou's autobiography, which celebrates Maya's body and
words, critiques the rape and racial oppression she suffers.

Maya finds, however, that her body and words exist uneasily together.
While in the early part of the narrative Maya depends heavily on literature,[33] in the text's final San Francisco section, all words, particularly those
packaged as literature, fail to account for her adolescent body's changes.
Reading Radclyffe Hall's *The Well of Loneliness* (1928) leads Maya to mistakenly
interpret these changes as signals that she is becoming a lesbian. When
Maya confronts her mother with this fear, Angelou further demonstrates
the inability of the verbal to explain the physical. Vivian's requiring Maya
to read aloud the dictionary definition of the word "vulva" echoes
strangely Flowers's asking Maya to read aloud from Dickens. Unlike Dickens's prose, however, Noah Webster's and Vivian's words lose their sooth-
ing power as soon as Maya is confronted with a stronger physical reality—
her own admiration for her girlfriend's fully developed breasts. This scene
in which Maya shifts her attention from words to bodies paves the way for
Angelou's concluding celebration of the black female body.

Seeking physical rather than verbal knowledge of her sexuality, Maya
determines to have sex with one of "the most eligible young men in the
neighborhood" (239). Their encounter, which "is unredeemed by shared
tenderness" (240), leaves sixteen-year-old Maya pregnant and alone. The
young man quits talking to her in her fourth month, and Maya's brother,
who is overseas, advises her not to tell her parents until she graduates from
high school. Yet it would be wrong to see Maya's motherhood as "a tragic
way to end the book and begin life as an adult."[34] While Angelou portrays

the pain and confusion resulting from Maya's pregnancy, she places a far greater emphasis on her newfound autonomy. Even Maya's naive style of seduction accentuates her feminist stance. She asks the young man, "Would you like to have a sexual intercourse with me?" (239). In posing this straightforward question, Maya claims control of her body and her identity for the first time in the text. Just as Jacobs describes Brent's union with Sands as a union of her body and will, Angelou celebrates Maya's encounter with the young man. She accentuates Maya's reclamation of her body and volition by ironically alluding to the violation she suffered as an eight-year-old. "Thanks to Mr. Freeman nine years before," asserts Angelou, "I had had no pain of entry to endure" (240).

By detailing how the pregnant Maya copes with her isolation, Angelou pays further tribute to Maya's increased autonomy and acceptance of her own body. Beginning to reject the literary myths that led her to deny her own agency, Maya accepts complete responsibility for her pregnancy: "For eons, it seemed, I had accepted my plight as the hapless, put-upon victim of fate and the Furies, but this time I had to face the fact that I had brought my new catastrophe upon myself" (241). This acceptance of responsibility also leads Maya to a greater acceptance of her own body's powers: "I had a baby. He was beautiful and mine. Totally mine. No one had bought him for me. No one had helped me endure the sickly gray months. I had had help in the child's conception, but no one could deny that I had had an immaculate pregnancy" (245). Angelou's use of the word "immaculate" not only challenges racist stereotypes that associate black women with illicit sexuality, but it also suggests that Maya has shed her earlier conceptions of her body as "dirty like mud" (2) and "shit-colored" (17). Because the eight-year-old Maya perceives her own mother as looking like the "Virgin Mary" (57), the word "immaculate" also indicates that the teenage Maya begins to see in herself the power and beauty she sees in Vivian.

Maya's lack of confidence in her body briefly returns, however, in the autobiography's final paragraphs. Vivian's suggestion that Maya sleep with her child accentuates her worry that she is too clumsy to handle a baby. Vivian banishes this fear by waking Maya and showing her the baby sleeping under a tent that Maya unconsciously formed with her body and a blanket. "See," Vivian whispers, "you don't have to think about doing the right thing. If you're for the right thing then you do it without thinking" (246). Presenting the mother/child bond as a symbol of Maya's newfound autonomy, this closing scene reverses her earlier privileging of the verbal over the physical and celebrates the harmonious interaction of her body and will.

Rape can destroy a woman's autonomy and self-image, yet Jacobs and Angelou transform this potentially destructive event into an opportunity to celebrate their resistance to somatophobia and negative stereotypes about the black female body. An early scene in *Caged Bird* serves as a synecdoche for the reembodiment both Angelou and Jacobs accomplish in recording their experiences of rape. Three "powhitetrash" girls ape the posture and singing of Maya's grandmother, yet she emerges victorious and beautiful from this degradation and calms the enraged Maya. Afterward Maya rakes away the girls' footprints in the lawn and creates a new pattern: "a large heart with lots of hearts growing smaller inside, and piercing from the outside rim to the smallest heart was an arrow" (27). These connected hearts, which represent the bond between Maya and her grandmother, encapsulate Angelou's and Jacobs's celebration of black motherhood as a sign of personal autonomy. In the grandmother's triumph over the white girls who mock and caricature her body, and in young Maya's erasure of their footprints, I see Angelou's and Jacobs's refutation of negative stereotypes about their bodies. Maya's newly raked pattern resembles their autobiographies—their writings (or rightings) of the black female body outside of dominant cultural definitions.

Notes

1. Susan Stanford Friedman, "Women's Autobiographical Selves: Theory and Practice," in *The Private Self: Theory and Practice of Women's Autobiographical Writings*, ed. Shari Benstock (Chapel Hill: Univ. of North Carolina Press, 1988), 37.

2. Susan Griffin argues that even the fear of rape causes women to negate their bodies: "The fear of rape permeates our lives. . . . the best defense against this is not to be, to deny being in the body." See *Rape: The Power Of Consciousness* (New York: Harper, 1979), qtd. in Jacquelyn Dowd Hall, "'The Mind That Burns in Each Body': Women, Rape, and Racial Violence," in *Powers of Desire: The Politics of Sexuality*, ed. Ann Snitow, Christine Stansell, and Sharon Thompson (New York: Monthly Review Press, 1983), 333.

3. Elizabeth V. Spelman, *Inessential Woman: Problems of Exclusion in Feminist Thought* (Boston: Beacon Press, 1988), 30, 126–31. While I assume that disdain for the female body is inherent in patriarchal ideology, I do not perceive this ideology as monolithic, and I discuss somatophobia's differing manifestations in Shakespeare's, Harriet Jacobs's, and Maya Angelou's times.

4. Ian Donaldson provides a detailed analysis of the role of the Lucretia myth in Samuel Richardson's *Clarissa* (1747–48), a novel that greatly influenced American novels of seduction before and during Jacobs's time. See *The Rapes of Lucretia: A Myth and Its Transformations* (Oxford: Clarendon, 1982), 57–82.

5. William Shakespeare, *The Poems*, ed. F. T. Prince (London: Methuen, 1974), 1655–56.

6. Stephanie H. Jed, *Chaste Thinking: The Rape of Lucretia and the Birth of Humanism* (Bloomington: Indiana Univ. Press, 1989), 13.

7. Shakespeare, 1184–90. Shakespeare's sources similarly privilege an integral self over the body.

8. There are many good feminist readings of *Lucrece*. My reading is most influenced by Coppelia Kahn, "The Rape in Shakespeare's *Lucrece*," *Shakespeare Studies* 9 (1976): 45–72.

9. Spelman, 126–32.

10. Darlene Clark Hine, "Rape and the Inner Lives of Black Women in the Middle West: Preliminary Thoughts on the Culture of Dissemblance," *Signs* 14 (1989): 917–20. In examining dissemblance, Hine also states that antebellum black women had to "collectively create alternative self-images and shield from scrutiny these private empowering definitions of self" in order to function in white patriarchal America (916). I will show how Jacobs and Angelou make their empowering self-definitions public in their autobiographies.

11. Because of the vast scholarship on negative stereotypes about the black woman's body, I will cite only those works that most strongly informed this essay. bell hooks, *Ain't I a Woman: Black Women and Feminism* (Boston: South End Press, 1981), 15–86; Angela Y. Davis, *Women, Race and Class* (New York: Random House, 1981); Hazel V. Carby, *Reconstructing Womanhood: The Emergence of the Afro-American Woman Novelist* (New York: Oxford Univ. Press, 1987), 20–61; Barbara Christian, *Black Feminist Criticism: Perspectives on Black Women Writers* (New York: Pergamon Press, 1985), 1–30; Christian, *Black Women Novelists: The Development of a Tradition, 1892–1976* (Westport: Greenwood Press, 1980); Sondra O'Neale, "Inhibiting Midwives, Usurping Creators: The Struggling Emergence of Black Women in American Fiction," in *Feminist Studies/Critical Studies,* ed. Teresa de Lauretis (Bloomington: Indiana Univ. Press, 1986), 139–56; Sander L. Gilman, "Black Bodies, White Bodies: Toward an Iconography of Female Sexuality in Late Nineteenth-Century Art, Medicine, and Literature," in *"Race," Writing, and Difference,* ed. Henry Louis Gates, Jr. (Chicago: Chicago Univ. Press, 1985), 223–61; Barbara Omolade, "Hearts of Darkness," in *Powers Of Desire: The Politics of Sexuality,* ed. Ann Snitow, Christine Stansell, and Sharon Thompson (New York: Monthly Review Press, 1983), 350–70; Frances Foster, "'In Respect to Females . . . ': Differences in the Portrayals of Women by Male and Female Narrators," *Black American Literature Forum* 15(1981): 66–70; Hall; and Hine.

12. hooks, *Talking Back: Thinking Feminist, Thinking Black* (Boston: South End Press, 1989), 140. hooks's challenge is indeed a difficult one. As Barbara Christian observes, "The garb of uninhibited passion wears better on a male, who after all, does not have to carry the burden of the race's morality or lack of it" (*Novelists*, 40).

13. All the names in Jacobs's text are pseudonyms. Dr. Flint is a fictitious

name for Jacobs's former master, James Norcom. In this paper I will refer to the author of the autobiography as Jacobs, and to the actor within it as Brent. In order to avoid confusion, I will call the other people Jacobs writes about by their pseudonyms.

14. For the basic tenets of "true womanhood" see Barbara Welter, *Dimity Convictions: The American Woman in the Nineteenth Century* (Columbus: Ohio Univ. Press, 1976), 21. For discussions of Jacobs's subversion of sentimental discourse see Carby, 20–61; Jean Fagan Yellin, "Texts and Contexts of Harriet Jacobs' *Incidents in the Life of a Slave Girl: Written by Herself*" in *The Slave's Narrative,* ed. Charles T. Davis and Henry Louis Gates, Jr. (New York: Oxford Univ. Press, 1985), 262–82; Yellin, introduction, *Incidents in the Life of a Slave Girl,* by Harriet Jacobs, ed. Yellin (Cambridge: Harvard Univ. Press, 1987), xiii–xxxiv; Valerie Smith, *Self-Discovery and Authority in Afro-American Narrative* (Cambridge: Harvard Univ. Press, 1987), 35–43; Joanne M. Braxton, "Harriet Jacobs' *Incidents in the Life of a Slave Girl:* The Re-Definition of the Slave Narrative Genre," *Massachusetts Review* 27 (1986): 379–87; Claudia Tate, "Allegories of Black Female Desire; or, Rereading Nineteenth-Century Sentimental Narratives of Black Female Authority," *Changing Our Own Words: Essays on Criticism, Theory, and Writing by Black Women* (New Brunswick: Rutgers Univ. Press, 1989), 108–11; and Mary Helen Washington, *Invented Lives: Narratives of Black Women 1860–1960* (Garden City: Doubleday, 1987), 3–15.

15. Susanna Rowson, *Charlotte Temple,* ed. Clara M. and Rudolf Kirk (New Haven: College and Univ. Press, 1964), 117. For an excellent discussion of how eighteenth-century English novels represented a split between the rape victim's body and mind see Frances Ferguson, "Rape and the Rise of the Novel," *Representations* 20 (1987): 88–110.

16. Welter, 23.

17. As Susan Staves observes, the idea of seduction is incomprehensible "if women have no rights over their own bodies but are simply the property of men to use as they will, as female slaves were the property of slaveowners." See "British Seduced Maidens," *Eighteenth-Century Studies* 14 (1981): 116.

18. Harriet Jacobs, *Incidents in the Life of a Slave Girl,* ed. Jean Fagan Yellin (Cambridge: Harvard Univ. Press, 1987), 27. Future references to this text will be inserted parenthetically.

19. William L. Andrews, "Dialogue in Antebellum Afro-American Autobiography," in *Studies in Autobiography,* ed. James Olney (New York: Oxford Univ. Press, 1988), 94. Braxton observes that Brent "uses 'sass' the way Frederick Douglass uses his fists and his feet, as a means of expressing her resistance" (386).

20. Carby's second chapter in *Reconstructing Womanhood,* "Slave and Mistress: Ideologies of Womanhood under Slavery" (20–39), is an excellent study of how nineteenth-century conceptions of "lady" and "womanhood" depended upon the exclusion of black women.

21. Carby, 57–59; Yellin, introduction, xxx–xxxi; Tate, 108–09; Washington, xxiii, 6–7.

22. Washington, xxiii.

23. Andrews, *To Tell a Free Story: The First Century of Afro-American Autobiography 1760–1865* (Urbana: Univ. of Chicago Press, 1986), 259.

24. For a discussion of how privileging a discrete spiritual realm increased patri-archal authority's control over the bodies of enslaved people and white women in antebellum America, see Karen Sanchez-Eppler, "Bodily Bonds: The Intersecting Rhetorics of Feminism and Abolition," *Representations* 24 (1988): 49–50.

25. Jane Tompkins, *Sensational Designs: The Cultural Work of American Fiction* (New York: Oxford Univ. Press, 1985), 150–51.

26. Valerie Smith, 32.

27. For discussions of Jacobs's depiction of her motherhood as a source of her personal autonomy, see Carby, 40–61; Tate, 107–10; and Braxton, *passim*.

28. Maya Angelou, *I Know Why the Caged Bird Sings* (New York: Bantam, 1969), 65. Future references to this text will be inserted parenthetically. I will refer to the au-thor of *Caged Bird* as Angelou, and to the actor within it as Maya. In my reading of the early part of Angelou's autobiography, I am indebted to Sidonie Smith's discus-sion of Maya's quest after her "self-accepted black womanhood," to Liliane K. Arensberg's analysis of Maya's dependence on books, and to Francoise Lionnet's ex-ploration of how Angelou makes her body the source and model of her creativity. See Smith, "The Song of the Caged Bird: Maya Angelou's Quest for Self-Accep-tance," *Southern Humanities Review* 7 (1973): 365–75; Arensberg, "Death as Metaphor of Self in *I Know Why the Caged Bird Sings,*" *CLA* 20 (1970): 275–76; Lionnet, *Autobiographical Voices: Race, Gender, Self-Portraiture* (Ithaca: Cornell Univ. Press, 1989), 130–68. I differ from these readers in that I discuss the somatophobia and racism in white literary discourse as significant obstacles that Maya must overcome before she can begin to recover from her rape and take pride in her body.

29. For another examination of this opening scene and for a consideration of Angelou's other images of flowing liquids and rhythms, see Lionnet, 134–35, 146. Unlike Lionnet, I emphasize Maya's attempts to control her body and words.

30. Christine Froula, "The Daughter's Seduction: Sexual Violence and Literary History," *Signs* 11 (1986): 673.

31. Shakespeare, 1498. He devotes over two hundred lines to Lucrece's viewing of this painting (1367–1569) and contrasts the muteness of the painted Hecuba with Lucrece's venting of grief and outrage at her rape:

> On this sad shadow [Hecuba] Lucrece spends her eyes,
> And shapes her sorrow to the beldame's woes,
> Who nothing wants to answer her but cries,

And bitter words to ban her cruel foes;
The painter was no god to lend her those,
    And therefore Lucrece swears he did her wrong,
    To give her so much grief, and not a tongue. (1457–64)

32. The following lines typify the many times Shakespeare makes this equation throughout his poem: "This heraldry in Lucrece' face was seen, / Argued by beauty's red and virtue's white" (64–65).

33. Arensberg, 275–76, and Lionnet, *passim.* Neither critic discusses Maya's dependence on literature in the San Francisco section of *Caged Bird.*

34. Stephanie A. Demetrakopoulos, "The Metaphysics of Matrilinearism in Women's Autobiography: Studies of Mead's *Blackberry Winter,* Hellman's *Pentimento,* Angelou's *I Know Why The Caged Bird Sings,* and Kingston's *The Woman Warrior,*" in *Women's Autobiography: Essays in Criticism,* ed. Estelle C. Jelinek (Bloomington: Indiana Univ. Press, 1980), 189.

Racial Protest, Identity, Words, and Form

PIERRE A. WALKER

◆ ◆ ◆

MAYA ANGELOU has told in interviews how Robert Loomis, her eventual Random House editor, goaded her into writing autobiography, teasing her with the challenge of writing *literary* autobiography. Considering herself a poet and playwright, she had repeatedly refused Loomis's requests that she write an autobiography until he told her that it was just as well: "He . . . said that to write an autobiograpby—as literature—is almost impossible. I said right then I'd do it" ("Maya Angelou," with Hitt, 211). Angelou often admits that she cannot resist a challenge; however, it was not the challenge of writing autobiography per se that Angelou could not resist (and that led to the 1970 publication of I *Know Why the Caged Bird Sings*) but the challenge implied in Loomis's remark about the difficulty of writing autobiography "as literature."[1]

Angelou does not elaborate on how she distinguishes literary autobiography from any other kind of autobiography, and of course, for a poststructuralist, the challenge to write *literary* rather than "ordinary" autobiography is meaningless because there is no difference between the two (see Eagleton, 201). For a formalist aesthetic, however, the distinctive qualities and characteristics of literary or poetic language as opposed to ordinary language are central operative concerns (see Brooks, 729–31; Shklovsky, 12; Fish, 68–96). Cleanth Brooks's belief that "the parts of a poem are related to each other organically, and related to the total theme indirectly" (730) was a primary tenet of interpretation for American New Critics, ultimately related to their determination to distinguish literary from ordinary language. Poststructuralism in its most vehemently antiformalist manifestations usually belittles Brooks's beliefs in organic unity and in the uniqueness of literary language, but criticisms of formalism and of "literature" as a distinct and privileged category, so typical of much poststructuralist theorizing, become specially problematic in relation to African-American literature.

Many African-American texts were written to create a particular political impact. As a result, one can hardly ignore either the political conditions in which the slave narratives and Richard Wright's early works, for example, were composed or the political impact their authors (and editors and publishers, at least of the slave narratives) intended them to have. Even African-American texts that are not obviously part of a protest tradition are received in a political context, as is clear from the tendency in much critical commentary on Zora Neale Hurston to demonstrate an elusive element of protest in her novels.

So important is the political to the experience of African-American literature that it comes as no surprise that the increasing incorporation of the African-American literary tradition into mainstream academic literary studies since 1980 coincides exactly with the increasingly greater significance of the political in the prevailing critical paradigm: what better for a political literary criticism to address than an overtly political literature?

The problem is that African-American literature has, on more than one occasion, relied on confirming its status as literature to accomplish its political aims. Since slavery relied on a belief that those enslaved were not really human beings, slave narrators responded by writing books that emphasized the fact that they themselves were humans who deserved to be treated as such. Since emancipation, African-American authors have used the same strategy to fight the belief in racial hierarchies that relegated them to second-class citizen status. One way to do this was to produce "high art," which was supposed to be one of the achievements of the highest orders of human civilization. African-American poetry provides many examples of this strategy: Claude McKay's and Countee Cullen's reliance on traditional, European poetic forms and James Weldon Johnson's "O Black and Unknown Bards." Cullen's "Yet Do I Marvel," for instance, relies on recognizable English "literary" features: Shakespearean sonnet form, rhyme, meter, references to Greek mythology, and the posing of a theological question as old as the Book of Job and as familiar as William Blake's "The Tyger."

Thus for a critical style to dismiss the closely related categories of form and of literature is to relegate to obscurity an important tradition of African-American literature and an important political tool of the struggle in the United States of Americans of African descent. This is clearly true in respect to *Caged Bird,* which displays the kind of literary unity that would please Brooks, but to the significant political end of demonstrating how to fight racism. Angelou wrote *Caged Bird* in the late 1960s at the height of the New Criticism, and therefore in order for it to be the *literary* autobiography Loomis referred to, Angelou's book had to display features considered at the time typical of literature, such as organic unity. This is a political gesture, since in creating a text that satisfies contemporary criteria of "high art," Angelou underscores one of the book's central themes: how undeservedly its protagonist was relegated to second-class citizenship in her early years. To ignore form in discussing Angelou's book, therefore, would mean ignoring a critical dimension of its important political work.

Because scholarly discussions of Angelou's autobiographical works have only appeared in any significant number in the last fifteen years, *Caged Bird* and her other books have avoided—or, depending on one's view, been spared—the kind of formal analysis typically associated with New Criticism or Structuralism.[2] Scholarly critics of *Caged Bird,* often influenced by feminist and African-American studies, have focused on such issues as whether the story of Angelou's young protagonist is personal or universal, or on race, gender, identity, displacement, or a combination of these. In relation to these issues, they discuss important episodes like the scene with the "powhitetrash" girls, young Maya's rape and subsequent muteness, her experience with Mrs. Flowers, the graduation, the visit to the dentist, Maya's month living in a junkyard, or her struggle to become a San Francisco streetcar conductor.[3] What they do not do is analyze these episodes as Angelou constructed them—often juxtaposing disparate incidents within an episode—and arranged and organized them, often undermining the chronology of her childhood story and juxtaposing the events of one chapter with the events of preceding and following ones so that they too comment on each other. The critics do not explore how Angelou, who has never denied the principle of selection in the writing of autobiography,[4] shaped the material of her childhood and adolescent life story in *Caged Bird* to present Maya's first sixteen years, much as a *bildungsroman* would, as a progressive process of affirming identity, learning about words, and resisting racism.[5] What scholars have focused on in *Caged Bird* does merit attention, but an attention to the formal strategies Angelou uses to emphasize what the book expresses about identity and race reveals a sequence of lessons about resisting racist oppression, a sequence that leads Maya progressively from helpless rage and indignation to forms of subtle resistance and finally to outright and active protest.

The progression from rage and indignation to subtle resistance to active protest gives *Caged Bird* a thematic unity that stands in contrast to the otherwise episodic quality of the narrative. To claim thematic unity is to argue that form and content work together, an assertion that is anathema to much current literary theory. However, the formal in *Caged Bird* is the vehicle of the political, and not analyzing this text formally can limit one's appreciation of how it intervenes in the political. Critics should not focus on the political at the expense of the formal but instead should see the political and the formal as inextricably related. Indeed, some of the most well-received works on American literature in the last decade offer compelling demonstrations of such a symbiosis of form and content. Jane Tompkins's *Sensational Designs* and Walter Benn Michaels's *The Gold Standard and the Logic of Naturalism,* for instance, are exemplary instances of new historicism or cultural criticism, but they nevertheless integrate virtuosic close formal analyses of literary texts into their overall projects.[6]

Caged Bird's commentators have discussed how episodic the book is, but these episodes are crafted much like short stories, and their arrangement throughout the book does not always follow strict chronology.[7] Nothing requires an autobiography to be chronological, but an expectation of chronology on the reader's part is normal in a text that begins, as *Caged Bird* does, with earliest memories. Nevertheless, one of the most important early episodes in *Caged Bird* comes much earlier in the book than it actually did in Angelou's life: the scene in which the "powhitetrash" girls taunt Maya's grandmother takes up the book's fifth chapter, but it occurred when Maya "was around ten years old" (23), two years after Mr. Freeman rapes her (which occurs in the twelfth chapter).

Situating the episode early in the book makes sense in the context of the previous chapters: the third chapter ends with Angelou describing her anger at the "used-to-be-sheriff" who warned her family of an impending Klan ride (14–15), and the fourth chapter ends with her meditation on her early inability to perceive white people as human (20–21). The scene with the "powhitetrash" girls follows this (24–27), indicating how nonhuman white people can be. But if that was all that motivated the organization of her episodes, Angelou could as easily have followed the meditation on white people's nonhumanity with the episode in which young Maya

breaks the china of her white employer, Mrs. Cullinan. What really organizes chapters three through five is Angelou's presentation of the futility
of indignation and the utility of subtle resistance as ways of responding to
racism. The scene with the ex-sheriff comes at the beginning of this sequence and only leaves Maya humiliated and angry:

> If on Judgment Day I were summoned by St. Peter to give testimony to the
> used-to-be sheriff's act of kindness, I would be unable to say anything in his
> behalf. His confidence that my uncle and every other Black man who heard
> of the Klan's coming ride would scurry under their houses to hide in
> chicken droppings was too humiliating to hear. (14)

The scene with the "powhitetrash" girls causes Maya to react with the
same helpless anger and humiliation, but through the response of her
grandmother Henderson (whom she calls Momma) to the girls' rudeness
and crudity, Maya learns there can be a better and more effective way to
respond.

At first, Maya's reaction to the "powhitetrash" girls is like her reaction
to the used-to-be sheriff: rage, indignation, humiliation, helplessness.
When the girls ape her grandmother's posture, Maya weeps, thinks of getting her uncle's rifle, and wants to throw lye and pepper on them and to
scream at them "that they were dirty, scummy peckerwoods" (24–25).
When they leave and Momma politely calls good-bye to them, Maya's rage
peaks:

> I burst. A firecracker July-the-Fourth burst. How could Momma call them
> Miz? The mean nasty things. Why couldn't she have come inside the sweet,
> cool store when we saw them breasting the hill? What did she prove? And
> then if they were dirty, mean and impudent, why did Momma have to call
> them Miz? (26)

But once the girls leave, young Maya realizes that her grandmother
has achieved something: "Something had happened out there, which I
couldn't completely understand. . . . Whatever the contest had been
out front, I knew Momma had won" (26–27). Angelou claims that her ten-
year-old self could not fully understand what had happened, though she
did understand that there had been a contest of wills and that her grandmother had won it.

The young girl can be only vaguely conscious of how to comprehend
the nature of the contest, but her next act and the organization of the
whole chapter indicate nonetheless how readers should comprehend it.
Angelou's description of the "powhitetrash" girls emphasizes their dirti-

ness. They are "grimy, snotty-nosed girls" (23), and "the dirt of [their] cotton dresses continued on their legs, feet, arms and faces to make them all of a piece" (25). In contrast to this, Maya's household is a model of cleanliness. The first thing Momma tells Maya after the "powhitetrash" girls have left is to wash her face (26). This seems appropriate because of how much Maya had been crying, but its real significance is apparent when considered in the context of the chapter's beginning and of what Maya does at the end of the chapter. The chapter begins: "'Thou shall not be dirty' and 'Thou shall not be impudent' were the two commandments of Grandmother Henderson upon which hung our total salvation," and the two subsequent paragraphs recount the ends to which Momma went to ensure her grandchildren's cleanliness (21). At first glance, this would appear to have nothing to do with the pain and humiliation of racism. But what the entire chapter demonstrates and what the ten-year-old Maya vaguely understands is that cleanliness, racism, and her grandmother's "victory" over the "powhitetrash" girls have everything to do with each other. Maya would seem to have understood this—even though the adult Angelou claims she did not—for once she has washed her face, without being told to do so, she rakes the trampled front yard into a pattern that her grandmother calls "right pretty" (27).[8]

Maya and Momma demonstrate that, unlike the white trash girls, *they* are neither dirty nor impudent. This is where the victory lies. Part of it consists of Momma's resisting the white girls' attempts to goad her into descending to their level of impudence. But another part of the victory lies in maintaining personal dignity through the symbolic importance of cleanliness and politeness. The victory itself will not bring about the downfall of segregation (which is perhaps why some critics see Grandmother Henderson as ultimately helpless against racist oppression [see Kent, 76; and Neubauer, 118]), but it does allow Momma and Maya to be proud of themselves. By demonstrating their own cleanliness and politeness, Maya and her grandmother establish their family's respectability in the face of racism and subtly throw the attempt to degrade them back on their oppressors. Furthermore, there is a more effective strategy for reacting to racism and segregation than rage and indignation—a strategy of subtle resistance, what Dolly McPherson calls "the dignified course of silent endurance" (33). Later episodes demonstrate the limitations of subtle resistance, but one should not underestimate its powers: without risking harm to life, liberty, or property, Momma is able to preserve her human dignity in the face of the white girls' attempts to belittle her. It may be all that she can do in the segregated South at the time, but it is something. What is more, as Angelou subsequently shows, it serves as a basis from which Maya can later move to protesting and combating racism actively.

An important feature of the chapter is that Angelou organizes it like a short story. It begins where it ends, with cleanliness and raking the yard bracketing the scene with the white trash girls, and it leaves the reader to work out the relationship between the confrontation with the girls and the cleaning of the yard. Because of this organization, the chapter becomes more than just a narration of bigoted behavior and Momma's and Maya's responses to it: "Such experiences," says McPherson, "are recorded not simply as historical events, but as symbolic revelations of Angelou's inner world" (49). The "powhitetrash" chapter takes on the additional dimension of a lesson in the utility of endowing everyday activities such as washing, raking a yard, or minding one's manners with symbolic value as a way of resisting bigotry. Making every minute of the day a symbolic means of fighting segregation in turn means that segregation is not a helpless and hopeless situation.

Angelou organizes the fifteenth chapter, the one about Mrs. Flowers, in a similarly tight fashion, interrelating the themes of racial pride, identity, and the power of words that run throughout. The positive effect that the attention of the elegant Mrs. Flowers has on the insecurity and identity crisis of young Maya is obvious.[9] By helping Maya to begin to have some self-confidence, Mrs. Flowers contributes to the young girl's affirmation of her identity: "I was liked, and what a difference it made. I was respected . . . for just being Marguerite Johnson. . . . She had made tea cookies for *me* and read to *me* from her favorite book" (85). Such respect and affection from an older person Maya admired surely had an important positive effect on a young girl suffering from the guilt and self-loathing that resulted from being raped by her mother's boyfriend. It is no wonder Angelou feels that Mrs. Flowers "threw me my first life line" (77).

While the Mrs. Flowers chapter seems, at first glance, not to have much to do with the politics of racism, this important step in Maya's sense of identity has everything to do with race. Since she had been twice sent away by her parents to live with her grandmother, it is no surprise that Maya had an insecurity and identity problem. In the opening pages of the book, Maya suffered from a strong case of racial self-hatred, fantasizing that she was "really white," with "light-blue eyes" and "long and blond" hair (2). At that point, Maya entirely separates her sense of self from her sense of race, and this is part of her identity crisis, since she refuses to accept being who she is and hankers after a foreign identity that is a compound of received ideas of white feminine beauty. By the end of the book, the opposite is the case. When the white secretary of the San Francisco streetcar company repeatedly frustrates her attempts for a job interview, Maya is at first tempted not to take it personally: "The incident was a recurring dream, concocted years before by stupid whites . . . I went further than forgiving the clerk, I accepted her as a fellow victim of the same puppeteer." But then Maya decides that the rebuffs, which have everything to do with her race, also have everything to do with her personally, and this is because her personal identity and her racial identity cannot be entirely separated: "The whole charade we had played out in that crummy waiting room had directly to do with me, Black, and her, white" (227). Attaining the streetcar conductor's job becomes not only a victory for civil rights, as a result, but also a personal victory for Maya's sense of self. One of the crucial transition points in this evolution over the course of the entire book from the total separation of self-image and race to the connection of the two comes in the Mrs. Flowers chapter, for not only does Mrs. Flowers make Maya feel liked and respected, but "she made me proud to be Negro, just by being herself" (79).[10] This is the first statement of black racial pride in the book, but others appear later: Joe Louis's victory, which "proved that we were the strongest people in the world" (115), and Maya's conclusion at the end of the graduation scene that "I was a proud member of the wonderful, beautiful Negro race" (156).

The Mrs. Flowers chapter emphasizes black racial pride by combining two apparently disparate episodes on the basis of their thematic affinity, much as the "powhitetrash" chapter did. Here the affinity is not cleanliness but the power of words, a theme central to African-American autobiography from the slave narratives to Richard Wright's *Black Boy* and beyond. The importance of the power of words, in themselves and in poetry, and, by implication, the importance of literature run throughout *Caged Bird*,[11] especially after the rape, when Maya fears that her lie at Mr. Freeman's trial caused his death. *Black Boy* demonstrates the negative power of words each time Wright is abused for not saying the right thing,[12] yet the book concludes on a positive note when Wright realizes that he can harness the power of words to his own artistic and political ends. Much the same thing happens in *Caged Bird*. Maya refuses to speak because she fears the potentially fatal power of words, but throughout the second half of the book she acknowledges that the imagination can harness the power of words to great ends. One of the high points in this realization comes at the end of the graduation scene, when the audience, having been insulted by a white guest speaker, lifts its morale by singing James Weldon Johnson's "Lift Ev'ry Voice and Sing" (155). Maya realizes that she "had never heard it before. Never heard the words, despite the thousands of times I had sung them," and this leads her to appreciate the African-American poetic tradition as she never had before. Angelou expresses that appreciation with an allusion to another Johnson poem: "Oh, Black known and unknown poets, how often have your auctioned pains sustained us? Who will compute the lonely nights made less lonely by your songs, or by the empty pots made less tragic by your tales?" (156). Because Johnson's words, like Angelou's story, are gathered "from the stuff of the black experience, with its suffering and its survival," to use Keneth Kinnamon's words, the singing of "Lift Ev'ry Voice and Sing" at the end of the graduation episode "is a paradigm of Angelou's own artistic endeavor in *I Know Why the Caged Bird Sings*" (132–33).

Mrs. Flowers lays the groundwork for this later appreciation of the power of the poetic word by explicitly stating the lesson of the positive power of words in her conversation with the ten-year-old Maya. (Her message is further emphasized because the main point of her invitation and attention to the mute girl is to convince her to use words again.) "[B]ear in mind," Mrs. Flowers tells Maya, "language is man's way of communicating with his fellow man and it is language alone that separates him from the lower animals. . . . Words mean more than what is set down on paper. It takes the human voice to infuse them with the shades of deeper meaning" (82). Mrs. Flowers's speech and her reading from Dickens themselves make Maya appreciate poetry—"I heard poetry for the first time in my life" (84), she says about Mrs. Flowers's reading—and the spoken word, but Angelou arranges the entire chapter to emphasize the power of words. The chapter begins with a description of Mrs. Flowers and her elegant command of standard English, which contrasts in their conversations with Momma's heavy dialect, much to Maya's shame: "Shame made me want to hide my face. . . . Momma left out the verb. Why not ask, 'How *are* you, *Mrs. Flowers?*' . . . 'Brother and Sister Wilcox is sho'ly the meanest—' 'Is,' Momma? 'Is'? Oh, please, not 'is,' Momma, for two or more" (78–79). As a result, Angelou has focused the chapter on the importance of words and their pronunciation, even in its very first pages, before Maya enters Mrs. Flowers's house.

The chapter's end, after Maya returns from her visit, also emphasizes the importance of words, this time in contrast to the way white people use words. When Maya tells her brother, "By the way, Bailey, Mrs. Flowers sent you some tea cookies—," Momma threatens to beat her granddaughter (85). The crime is that since "Jesus was the Way, the Truth and the Light," saying "by the way" was, in Momma's view, blasphemous (86). This episode would seem thematically unrelated to the rest of the chapter and only an example of Momma's domestic theocracy were it not for the chapter's final sentence: "When Bailey tried to interpret the words with: 'Whitefolks use "by the way" to mean while we're on the subject,' Momma reminded us that 'whitefolks' mouths were most in general loose and their words were an abomination before Christ'" (86–87). While the "by the way" episode concludes the chapter, *Black Boy* fashion, with an example of the awful power of words, this final sentence concludes both the episode and chapter just as the emphasis on cleanliness concluded the "powhitetrash" chapter: through their greater attention to details, the Henderson/Johnson clan shows itself to be superior to whites; and instead of showing Momma to be abusive and tyrannic, the "by the way" episode anticipates the affirmation later in the book of the strength blacks find in the careful—even poetic—use of words, just as Mrs. Flowers does in her reading and in her speech about words.

The internal organization of chapters, as in the "powhitetrash" and Mrs. Flowers chapters, into thematic units that would make Cleanth Brooks proud is but one of the effects Angelou uses in *Caged Bird*. Equally effective is the way Angelou juxtaposes chapters. For example, she follows the Mrs. Flowers chapter, with its lessons on the power of words and on identity, with the chapter (the sixteenth) in which Maya breaks Mrs. Cullinan's dishes because the white employer neglects to take a single but important word—Maya's name—and Maya's identity seriously. This chapter comments, then, on the previous one by showing Maya acting on the basis of what she has learned in the previous chapter about the importance of words and about affirming identity. Maya's smashing of the dishes is also an important stage in the progression of strategies for responding to racial oppression from helpless indignation to subtle resistance to active protest. No longer helplessly angered and humiliated as she was by the former sheriff and the white girls taunting her grandmother, Maya shows in the Mrs. Cullinan chapter that she has internalized the lesson of the "powhitetrash" episode and can figure out, with her brother's advice, a way to resist her white employer's demeaning of her that is subtle and yet allows her to feel herself the victor of an unspoken confrontation. After Mrs. Cullinan insists on calling her Mary instead of Margaret (which best approximates her real name, Marguerite), Maya realizes that she can neither correct her employer nor simply quit the job. Like her grandmother with the rude white girls, Maya cannot openly confront her oppressor, nor can she allow the situation to continue. Instead she breaks Mrs. Cullinan's favorite dishes and walks out, exulting as Mrs.

Cullinan tells her guests, "Her name's Margaret, goddamn it, her name's Margaret!" (93)[13]

Angelou follows this chapter with a series of three chapters, the seventeenth through the nineteenth, each of which depicts subtle black resistance to white oppression. However, while the sixteenth chapter ends with Maya exulting at the efficacy of her resistance to Mrs. Cullinan, these chapters increasingly express the limitations of subtle resistance. The seventeenth chapter tells about Maya's and Bailey's viewing movies starring Kay Francis, who resembles their mother, and describes how Maya turns the stereotypical depiction of black people in Hollywood movies back onto the unknowing white members of the audience. As the whites snicker at the Stepin Fetchit-like black chauffeur in one Kay Francis comedy, Maya turns the joke on them:

> I laughed too, but not at the hateful jokes. . . . I laughed because, except that she was white, the big movie star looked just like my mother. Except that she lived in a big mansion with a thousand servants, she lived just like my mother. And it was funny to think of the whitefolks' not knowing that the woman they were adoring could be my mother's twin, except that she was white and my mother was prettier. Much prettier. (99–100)

This passage works very much like Momma's victory over the white trash girls: the whites' taunts are turned back on them, though the whites may not know it. Nonetheless, this permits the black person to feel superior instead of humiliated while avoiding the kind of open confrontation that could lead to violence. What is problematic about the seventeenth chapter is that, as in the eighteenth and nineteenth chapters, the end of the chapter casts a shadow on the success achieved in the moment of subtle resistance by describing Bailey's very different reaction to the movie: it makes him sullen, and on their way home, he terrifies Maya by running in front of an oncoming train (100).

In the eighteenth and nineteenth chapters, which tell about the revival meeting and the Joe Louis fight, a black community is able to feel superior to whites. Both chapters, though, end ambiguously, with a reminder that the feeling of superiority is transitory and fragile. At the revival, the congregation thrills to a sermon that subtly accuses whites of lacking charity while reminding the congregation about the ultimate reward for their true charity. The congregation leaves the revival feeling "it was better to be meek and lowly, spat upon and abused for this little time than to spend eternity frying in the fires of hell" (110–11). Again, the oppressed are able to feel superior without risking the violence of an open confrontation. The final two paragraphs of the chapter, however, compare the gospel music at the revival with the "ragged sound" of the "barrelhouse blues" coming from the honky-tonk run by "Miss Grace, the good-time woman" (111). Like the parishioners at the revival, the customers of the suitably named Miss Grace "had forsaken their own distress for a little while." However, "reality began its tedious crawl back into their reasoning. After all, they were needy and hungry and despised and dispossessed, and sinners the world over were in the driver's seat. How long, merciful Father? How long? . . . All asked the same questions. How long, oh God? How long?" (111). Whereas the "powhitetrash" and Mrs. Cullinan chapters ended on a note of victory, this chapter ends on one that rings more of defeat. This is because the book moves through the three strategies for responding to white racist oppression—helpless indignation, subtle resistance, and active protest—and at this point is preparing the transition from the limited victories of subtle resistance to the outright victory of active protest.

The next chapter, the nineteenth, which describes the community at the store listening to a Joe Louis match, follows the same pattern as the revival chapter. Louis's victory provides his fans a stirring moment of racial pride and exaltation: "Champion of the world. A Black boy. Some Black mother's son. He was the strongest man in the world. People drank Coca-Colas like ambrosia and ate candy bars like Christmas" (114). But while Louis's victory allows his black fans to feel themselves stronger than and superior to their white oppressors, there are limits to how far the black community can rejoice in its superiority. The chapter ends by mentioning that those who lived far out of town spent the night with friends in town because "it wouldn't do for a Black man and his family to be caught on a lonely country road on a night when Joe Louis had proved that we were the strongest people in the world" (115).

Because chapters eighteen and nineteen explore the limits to subtle but passive resistance, the book has to go on to present other possible ways of responding to white oppression. The climactic response, one that consists of active resistance and outright protest, is Maya's persisting and breaking the color line of the San Francisco streetcar company, described in the thirty-fourth chapter. Since *Caged Bird* was written in the late sixties, at the height of the black power movement and at a time that was still debating the value of Martin Luther King's belief in nonviolent protest, it is no surprise that this act of protest is the climactic moment of resistance to white oppression in the book, a moment that says: Momma's type of resistance was fine in its time and place, but now it is time for some real action.[14] There are at least three other episodes in the second half of *Caged Bird,* however, that explore the line between subtle but passive resistance and active, open protest: the graduation scene (chapter twenty-three), the dentist scene (chapter twenty-four), and the story Daddy Clidell's friend, Red Leg, tells about double-crossing a white con man (chapter twenty-nine).

Falling as they do between the Joe Louis chapter and the San Francisco streetcar company chapter, these three episodes chart the transition from subtle resistance to active protest. The graduation scene for the most part follows the early, entirely positive examples of subtle resistance in *Caged Bird*. The only difference is that the resistance is no longer so subtle and that it specifically takes the form of poetry, which in itself valorizes the African-American literary tradition as a source for resisting white racist oppression. Otherwise, the graduation chapter conforms to the pattern established by the "powhitetrash" and Mrs. Cullinan chapters: first, there is the insult by the white person, when the speaker tells the black audience about all the improvements that the white school will receive—improvements that far surpass the few scheduled for the black school (151). There is Maya's first response of humiliation and anger: "Then I wished that Gabriel Prosser and Nat Turner had killed all whitefolks in their beds" (152), shared now by the community: "[T]he proud graduating class of 1940 had dropped their heads" (152). Then there is the action on the part of a member of the black community—Henry Reed's improvised leading the audience in "Lift Ev'ry Voice and Sing" (155)—that at the same time avoids an irreversible confrontation with the white oppressor and permits the black community to feel its dignity and superiority: "We were on top again. As always, again. We survived" (156).

The primary difference in the graduation chapter is that because the audience sings together, the resistance is a community action. The resistance is still not exactly an outright protest, and it still avoids open confrontation since the white insulter has left and does not hear the singing. Otherwise, the scene resembles a civil rights protest two decades later. The graduation also serves as an introduction for the dentist chapter, which is similar to the graduation chapter because of the way it highlights literature as a possible source for resisting racist oppression, and which is the crucial transitional chapter from subtle resistance to active protest because it opens the door to the eventuality of open confrontation by presenting the closest instance in the book of a black person in Stamps openly confronting a racist white.

The insult in the dentist chapter occurs when Stamps's white and only dentist—to whom Maya's grandmother had lent money, interest-free and as a favor—refuses to treat Maya's excruciating toothache, telling Maya and Momma, "[M]y policy is I'd rather stick my hand in a dog's mouth than in a nigger's" (160). From this point on, though, the chapter ceases to follow the pattern of the previous examples of resistance. Instead, Momma leaves Maya in the alley behind the dentist's office and, in a passage printed in italics, enters the office transformed into a superwoman and threatens to run the now-trembling dentist out of town. Readers quickly perceive that this passage is italicized because it is Maya's fantasy, but they do have to read a few sentences of the fantasy before realizing it. The chapter ends, after Maya and Momma travel to the black dentist in Texarkana, with Angelou's explanation of what really happened inside the white dentist's office—Momma collected interest on her loan to the dentist, which pays the bus fare to Texarkana—and Angelou's remark: "I preferred, much preferred, my version" (164).

The fantasy scene bears attention because it is the only one like it in *Caged Bird.* It is the only italicized passage in the book and the only one that confuses the reader—even if only for a moment—over what is real and what is fantasy. Some critics have argued that this passage serves the purpose of underlining how limited Momma's ability to fight racism is,[15] and it is true that in a better world, Momma would have been able to exact proper and courteous care from a dentist who was beholden to her. This reading, however, does not account for either the uniqueness of the presentation of the passage or the very real pride Maya feels for her grandmother as they ride the bus between Stamps and Texarkana: "I was so proud of being her granddaughter and sure that some of her magic must have come down to me" (162–63). On the one hand, the italicized passage does highlight the contrast between what Maya wishes her grandmother could do to a racist with what little she can do, thus again demonstrating the limitations of subtle resistance as an overall strategy for responding to racist oppression. On the other hand, the fantasy passage anticipates the kind of outright confrontations between oppressed black and racist oppressor that occurred when Maya broke the streetcar company's color line and in the civil rights movement. Although it is only a fantasy, it is the first instance in *Caged Bird* of a black person openly confronting a racist white and thus is the first hint that such confrontation is a possibility.

The fact that the fantasy passage is an act of imagination is also significant, since it hints that imagination and storytelling can be forms of resisting racism. It is natural to read the fantasy passage in this way because of its placement immediately after the apostrophe to "Black known and unknown poets" at the end of the graduation chapter (156). Because of this passage praising black poets, we are all the more inclined to see the imagined, italicized fantasy passage five pages later as itself an instance of poetry. For one, the apostrophe includes in the category of "poets" anyone who uses the power of the word—"include preachers, musicians and blues singers" (156). Thus, anyone who uses language to describe pain and suffering and their causes (i.e., blues singers) belongs in the category of poets. According to this definition, the author of *I Know Why the Caged Bird Sings* is a blues singer, and therefore a poet, too, since telling why the caged bird sings is an instance of describing pain and suffering and their causes, an instance of the blues. Loosely defined, poetry is also an act of imagination, and thus the italicized fantasy passage in the dentist chapter is poetic since it is an act of imagination. In fact, it is the first instance of Maya being a poet and thus the first step toward the far more monumental act of writing *I Know Why the Caged Bird Sings* itself. Poetry, in all its forms, can be an act of resistance. The graduation chapter has already made that clear, but the dentist chapter makes it clear that the victim of racial oppression can herself become a poet and use *her* poetry as a form of resistance. Maya had begun to learn the positive power of poetry and of words in the Mrs. Flowers chapter. Now she begins the process of harnessing the power of words to positive effect, a process that concludes with the composition almost thirty years later of the very book in hand.

The final instance of not-quite-outright resistance is the scam Red Leg tells (in chapter twenty-nine) about pulling on a white con man. This episode is not the open, active protest of Maya's integration of the streetcars since it does not involve a direct confrontation with the white racist, but it is closer to it than any of the previous examples of resistance because the white person ends up knowing that he has been had at his own game. The inclusion of the episode is at first glance irrelevant to the heroine's personal development, but Angelou's comments at the end of the chapter make clear how the passage fits with the rest of the book. For one, Angelou remarks, "It wasn't possible for me to regard [Red Leg and his accomplice] as criminals or be anything but proud of their achievements" (190). The reason for her pride is that these black con artists are achieving revenge for wrongs incurred against the entire race: "We are the victims of the world's most comprehensive robbery. Life demands a balance. It's all right if we do a little robbing now" (190–91). The scam is, therefore, another example of fighting back against white domination and racist oppression, an example that, like the others, meets with the author's approval.

The scam artist chapter ends, like so many other chapters, with a paragraph that appears to have little to do with what precedes. It tells about how Maya and her black schoolmates learned to use Standard English and dialect in their appropriate settings. This short paragraph certainly belongs to the commentary running throughout the book on appreciating the significance and power of words: "We were alert to the gap separating the written word from the colloquial" (191). It also serves to emphasize the superior ability of blacks to adapt to and get the best of circumstances and situations: "My education and that of my Black associates were quite different from the education of our white schoolmates. In the classroom we all learned past participles, but in the streets and in our homes the Blacks learned to drop *s*'s from plurals and suffixes from past-tense verbs" (191). Angelou shows here the superior adaptability of her black schoolmates (and that Maya has come a long way from her scorn of her grandmother's use of dialect): the blacks learn all the whites do and more. This lesson is entirely appropriate to the con artist chapter, since what the stories about pulling scams demonstrate is the black version of heroism, which is to make the most of what little one has—in other words, adaptability: "[I]n the Black American ghettos the hero is that man who is offered only the crumbs from his country's table but by ingenuity and courage is able to take for himself a Lucullan feast" (190).

Within strictly legal confines, such an ability is the essence of the American myth of success, and undoubtedly, at least part of the appeal of *Caged Bird* is that it corresponds both to this definition of black heroism and to the outline of a typical success story.[16] The product of a broken family, raped at age eight, Angelou was offered at first "only the crumbs" from her "country's table." She suffers from an inferiority complex, an identity crisis, and the humiliation of racist insults. By the end of the book, however, she no longer feels inferior, knows who she is, and knows that she can respond to racism in ways that preserve her dignity and her life, liberty, and property, and she knows—and demonstrates in addition through the very existence of the book itself—that she can respond by using the power of words. It may be impossible to convince a poststructuralist that there is something uniquely literary about Angelou's autobiography, but certainly part of what this autobiography is about is the power and utility of literature and its own genesis and existence as a protest against racism. One serves Angelou and *Caged Bird* better by emphasizing how form and political content work together. As Elizabeth Fox-Genovese says in respect to the general tradition of autobiographies by African-American women:

> The theoretical challenge lies in bringing sophisticated skills to the service of a politically informed reading of texts. To read well, to read fully, is in-

escapably to read politically, but to foreground the politics, as if these could somehow be distinguished from the reading itself, is to render the reading suspect. (67)

To neglect many of the formal ways *Caged Bird* expresses its points about identity, words, and race is to ignore the extent to which Angelou successfully met Loomis's challenge, an important aspect of her artistic accomplishment, and the potential utility of this text in literary classrooms, especially those that emphasize combining formal and ideologically based approaches to analyzing literature.

Notes

1. Angelou tells the story about how she came to write *I Know Why the Caged Bird Sings* in several interviews collected by Jeffrey M. Elliot (80, 151–52, 211). She admits having an inability to "resist a challenge" (*"Westways,"* 80) in her 1983 interview with Claudia Tate ("Maya Angelou," 151–52), and in at least two interviews she discusses James Baldwin's possible role in helping Loomis use her attraction to a challenge as a ploy to get her to agree to write an autobiography (*"Westways,"* 80; "Maya Angelou," with Tate, 151).

2. A search in the MLA computerized data bank reveals forty-four items on Angelou, with the oldest dating back to 1973, three years after the publication of *I Know Why the Caged Bird Sings.* Twenty-eight of these forty-four items have appeared since 1985, and only nine appeared before 1980 (and of these, two are interviews, one is bibliographic information, and one is a portion of a dissertation). There are different possibilities for interpreting these facts: on the one hand, it may be that scholarly critics have been slow to "catch up" to Angelou, slow to treat her work—and thus to recognize it—as literature worthy of their attention; on the other hand, it may be that the scholarly status of Angelou's work has risen in concert with poststructuralism's rise and has done so because poststructuralism has made it possible to appreciate Angelou's work in new ways.

3. For the significance of identity in *Caged Bird,* see Butterfield (203), Schmidt (25–27), McPherson (16, 18, 121), and Arensberg (275, 278–80, 288–90). On displacement, see Neubauer (117–19, 126–27) and Bloom (296–97). For a consideration of the personal vs. the universal, see McPherson (45–46), Cudjoe (10), O'Neale (26), McMurry (109), and Kinnamon, who stresses the importance of community in *Caged Bird* (123–33). On the "powhitetrash" scene, see Butterfield (210–12), McPherson (31–33), and McMurry (108). For an extensive consideration of the rape, see Froula (634–36). For the effect of the rape on Maya and her relationship with Mrs. Flowers, see Lionnet (147–52). For the graduation, see Butterfield (207), McMurry (109–10),

Arensberg (283), and Cudjoe (14). For the visit to the dentist, see Braxton (302–04) and Neubauer (118–19). For the month in the junkyard, see Gilbert (41) and Lionnet (156–57).

4. See Angelou's interviews with Tate ("Maya Angelou," 152) and with Neubauer ("Interview," 288–89). In an interview included in McPherson's *Order Out of Chaos,* Angelou mentions a number of incidents she omitted—some consciously, some unconsciously—from *Caged Bird* (138–40, 145–47, 157–58). O'Neale, who writes that Angelou's "narrative was held together by controlled techniques of artistic fiction" (26) and that her books are "arranged in loosely structured plot sequences which are skillfully controlled" (32), does not discuss these techniques or arrangements in any detail.

5. Angelou creates enough potential confusion about her protagonist's identity by having her called different names by different people—Ritie, Maya, Marguerite, Margaret, Mary, Sister. For the sake of consistency, I use the name "Maya" to refer to the protagonist of *Caged Bird* and the name "Angelou" to refer to its author.

6. Michaels's book is published in Stephen Greenblatt's series, "The New Historicism: Studies in Cultural Poetics," and Tompkins's book, whose subtitle is *The Cultural Work of American Fiction, 1790–1860,* emphasizes reading literature in its historical context. Tompkins's chapter, "Sentimental Power: *Uncle Tom's Cabin* and the Politics of Literary History," and Michaels's chapter on *McTeague* strike me as brilliant close literary analysis.

7. Schmidt (25) and McPherson (26) comment on the episodic quality of *Caged Bird.* Schmidt is the one commentator on *Caged Bird* to mention that "each reminiscence forms a unit" (25). An indication of how episodic *Caged Bird* is is how readily selections from it have lent themselves to being anthologized.

8. McMurry argues insightfully that Maya "is using the design [she rakes in the front yard] to organize feelings she could not otherwise order or express, just as Momma has used the song to organize her thoughts and feelings beyond the range of the children's taunts. She triumphs not only in spite of her restrictions, but because of them. It is because, as a Black woman, she must maintain the role of respect toward the white children that she discovers another vehicle for the true emotions" (108). Kinnamon, arguing that "Angelou's purpose is to portray cleanliness as a bonding ritual in black culture" (127), contrasts the importance of washing in the "powhitetrash" chapter with the scene in *Black Boy* in which Richard Wright tells about his grandmother's washing him.

9. See Bloom, who points to Mrs. Flowers as "a perceptive mother-substitute" (293). Sexual identity is central to the book's last two chapters, in which Angelou tells about Maya's concerns about her sexual identity and the birth of her son. For discussions of these last two chapters, see Smith (373–74), Buss (103–04), Schmidt

(26–27), McPherson (53–55), Arensberg (290–91), Butterfield (213), Lionnet (135–36), Demetrakopoulos (198–99), and MacKethan (60).

10. By being herself, Mrs. Flowers made Maya proud of her racial background, "proud to be Negro," but the real lesson Maya needs to learn is double: by being herself, Maya herself can be "proud to be Negro," and by being "proud to be Negro," Maya can be herself. Thus the language of the phrase implies the link between being "proud to be Negro" and being oneself.

11. See MacKethan, who emphasizes "verbal humor as a survival strategy" in *Caged Bird*. Cudjoe, arguing that "speech and language became instruments of liberation in Afro-American thought," reads *Caged Bird* in the context of this important theme (10–11).

12. Examples of this abuse occur when Wright tells his grandmother to kiss his ass, when he nonchalantly answers his uncle's question about the time of day, or when a drunken white man bashes him in the face for forgetting to say "sir" (40–44, 149–53, 173–74).

13. Thanks to my colleague, Mark Richardson, for pointing out that in Sergei Eisenstein's *Potemkin* the sailors rebelled against their officers by smashing dishes and for implying that dish smashing as an act of rebellion may be a literary trope.

14. Angelou has spoken in at least two interviews about the importance of protest in her work ("*Zelo* Interviews Maya Angelou," 167; "The Maya Character," 198).

15. See, for example, Neubauer (118). Mary Jane Lupton also feels that in the dentist episode "the grandmother has been defeated and humiliated, her only reward a mere ten dollars in interest for a loan she had made to the dentist" (261).

16. On May 29, 1994, twenty-four years after *Caged Bird*'s initial publication, the paperback edition was in its sixty-seventh week on the *New York Times Book Review* list of paperback best sellers.

Works Cited

Angelou, Maya. "An Interview with Maya Angelou," with Carol E. Neubauer. *Massachusetts Review: A Quarterly of Literature, the Arts, and Public Affairs* 28 (1987): 286–92.

———. *I Know Why the Caged Bird Sings.* (New York: Bantam, 1971).

———. "Maya Angelou," with Claudia Tate. Elliot, 146–56.

———. "Maya Angelou," with Greg Hitt. Elliot, 205–13.

———. "The Maya Character," with Jackie Kay. Elliot, 194–200.

———. "*Westways* Women: Life Is for Living," with Judith Rich. Elliot, 77–85.

———. "*Zelo* Interviews Maya Angelou," with Russell Harris. Elliot, 165–72.

Arensberg, Liliane K. "Death as Metaphor of Self in *I Know Why the Caged Bird Sings.*" *College Language Association Journal* 20 (1976): 273–91.

Bloom, Lynn Z. "Heritages: Dimensions of Mother-Daughter Relationships in Women's Autobiographies," in *The Lost Tradition: Mothers and Daughters in Literature.* Ed. Cathy N. Davidson and E. M. Broner (New York: Ungar, 1980), 291–303.

Braxton, Joanne M. "Ancestral Presence: The Outraged Mother Figure in Contemporary Afra-American Writing," in *Wild Women in the Whirlwind: Afra-American Culture and the Contemporary Literary Renaissance.* Ed. Joanne M. Braxton and Andrée Nicola McLaughlin (New Brunswick: Rutgers Univ. Press, 1990), 299–315.

Brooks, Cleanth. "Irony as a Principle of Structure." 1948; rev. 1951. In *Literary Opinion in America: Essays Illustrating the Status, Methods, and Problems of Criticism in the United States in the Twentieth Century.* Ed. Morton Dauwen Zabel. Rev. ed. (New York: Harper, 1951), 729–41.

Buss, Helen M. "Reading for the Doubled Discourse of American Women's Autobiography." *A/B: Auto/Biography Studies* 6 (1991): 95–108.

Butterfield, Stephen. *Black Autobiography in America* (Amherst: Univ. of Massachusetts Press, 1974).

Cudjoe, Selwyn R. "Maya Angelou and the Autobiographical Statement," in *Black Women Writers (1950–1980): A Critical Evaluation.* Ed. Mari Evans (Garden City: Doubleday-Anchor, 1984), 6–24.

Cullen, Countee. "Yet Do I Marvel," in *The Black Poets.* Ed. Dudley Randall (New York: Bantam, 1971), 100.

Demetrakopoulos, Stephanie A. "The Metaphysics of Matrilinearism in Women's Autobiography: Studies of Mead's *Blackberry Winter,* Hellman's *Pentimento,* Angelou's *I Know Why the Caged Bird Sings,* and Kingston's *The Woman Warrior,*" in *Women's Autobiography: Essays in Criticism.* Ed. Estelle C. Jelinek (Bloomington: Indiana Univ. Press, 1980), 180–205.

Eagleton, Terry. *Literary Theory: An Introduction* (Minneapolis: Univ. of Minnesota Press, 1983).

Elliot, Jeffrey M., ed. *Conversations with Maya Angelou* (Jackson: Univ. Press of Mississippi, 1989).

Fish, Stanley. *Is There a Text in This Class? The Authority of Interpretive Communities* (Cambridge: Harvard Univ. Press, 1980).

Fox-Genovese, Elizabeth. "My Statue, My Self: Autobiographical Writings of Afro-American Women," in *The Private Self: Theory and Practice of Women's Autobiographical Writings.* Ed. Shari Benstock (Chapel Hill: Univ. of North Carolina Press, 1988), 63–89.

Froula, Christine. "The Daughter's Seduction: Sexual Violence and Literary History." *Signs: Journal of Women in Culture and Society* 11 (1986): 621–44.

Johnson, James Weldon. "O Black and Unknown Bards." *The Black Poets.* Ed. Dudley Randall (New York: Bantam, 1971), 42–43.

Kent, George E. "Maya Angelou's *I Know Why the Caged Bird Sings* and Black Autobiographical Tradition." *Kansas Quarterly* 7 (1975): 72–78.

Kinnamon, Keneth. "Call and Response: Intertextuality in Two Autobiographical Works by Richard Wright and Maya Angelou," in *Belief vs. Theory in Black American Literary Criticism.* Ed. Joe Weixlmann and Chester J. Fontenot (Greenwood: Penkevill, 1986), 121–34.

Lionnet, Françoise. *Autobiographical Voices: Race, Gender, Self-Portraiture* (Ithaca: Cornell Univ. Press, 1989).

Lupton, Mary Jane. "Singing the Black Mother: Maya Angelou and Autobiographical Continuity." *Black American Literature Forum* 24 (1990): 257–76.

MacKethan, Lucinda H. "Mother Wit: Humor in Afro-American Women's Autobiography." *Studies in American Humor* 4 (1985): 51–61.

McMurry, Myra K. "Role-Playing as Art in Maya Angelou's 'Caged Bird.'" *South Atlantic Bulletin* 41(1976): 106–11.

McPherson, Dolly A. *Order Out of Chaos: The Autobiographical Works of Maya Angelou* (New York: Peter Lang, 1990).

Michaels, Walter Benn. *The Gold Standard and the Logic of Naturalism: American Literature at the Turn of the Century* (Berkeley: Univ. of California Press, 1987).

Neubauer, Carol E. "Maya Angelou: Self and a Song of Freedom in the Southern Tradition," in *Southern Women Writers: The New Generation.* Ed. Tonette Bond Inge (Tuscaloosa: Univ. of Alabama Press, 1990), 114–42.

O'Neale, Sondra. "Reconstruction of the Composite Self: New Images of Black Women in Maya Angelou's Continuing Autobiography," in *Black Women Writers (1950–1980): A Critical Evaluation.* Ed. Mari Evans (Garden City: Doubleday-Anchor, 1984), 25–36.

Schmidt, Jan Zlotnik. "The Other: A Study of the Persona in Several Contemporary Women's Autobiographies." *The CEA Critic* 43, no.1 (1980): 24–31.

Shklovsky, Victor. "Art as Technique," in *Russian Formalist Criticism: Four Essays.* Ed. Lee T. Lemon and Marion J. Reis (Lincoln: Univ. of Nebraska Press, 1965), 3–24.

Smith, Sidonie Ann. "The Song of a Caged Bird: Maya Angelou's Quest after Self-Acceptance." *Southern Humanities Review* 7 (1973): 365–75.

Tompkins, Jane P. *Sensational Designs: The Cultural Work of American Fiction, 1790–1860.* (New York: Oxford Univ. Press, 1985).

Wright, Richard. *Black Boy (American Hunger). Later Works: Black Boy (American Hunger); The Outsider* (New York: Library of America, 1991).

Paths to Escape

SUSAN GILBERT

❖ ❖ ❖

M AYA ANGELOU'S FIRST autobiographical book, *I Know Why the Caged Bird Sings* (1970), opens in church on Easter Sunday with the child dressed up in a lavender taffeta dress lovingly tucked by "Momma," her grandmother. She hopes to wake from her "black ugly dream" to "look like one of the sweet little white girls who were everybody's dream of what was right with the world" (4). The book closes with the heroine, an unmarried sixteen-year-old mother, who has gazed on her beautiful baby, afraid to handle him, until the night her mother puts the baby in bed beside her. Though she fears she will roll over and crush him, Maya wakes to find him sleeping safely by her side under the tent of covers she has made with her arm. Her mother whispers comfortingly, "See, you don't have to think about doing the right thing. If you're for the right thing, then you do it without thinking" (281).

The writer neither wishes to be white nor fears for her black son. From the conflicts of black and white worlds and from the conflicts of styles of her rural religious grandmother and her streetwise urban mother, she has found the strengths that will lead her beyond them both. But she has not done it "without thinking." Between the years when she was the sixteen-year-old mother, in 1944, and when as a woman of forty-two, in 1970, she published her book, she did a great deal of thinking about "doing the right

thing" and did her thinking through a very varied career and wide experience of the world. The reader of the book must deal throughout with the
dual perspective of the child, growing to consciousness of herself and the
limits of her world, and the author, experienced, confident, and didactic.

It is a story of hurt and loneliness and anger and love. The first memory
is of separation: when she was three and her brother Bailey four, they were
sent alone by train from California, where their parents had broken up
their marriage, to Stamps, Arkansas, to live with their paternal grandmother. Fixed forever in the woman's consciousness are her love for her
beautiful, clever brother, their grief, and their dreams of the mother who
has sent them away. Intertwined with these memories is the enormous
presence of the grandmother, "Momma," a shopkeeper and a devout
Christian who prays morning and evening. By her faith she endures this
world, for whose injustice she has no explanation to give the children, and
hopes for her reward and retribution in the next world. The child sees and
the author remembers the crushing poverty of those farm workers who
trudge through Momma's store, hopeful and singing in the morning,
bone weary and no richer at evening.

The whites of Stamps live across town and appear in the earliest memories only in scattered terrible vignettes: of nights when the Klan rides and
all the black men hide, some in the chicken droppings under their homes,
her Uncle Willie in the bottom of a barrel of potatoes; of days when
"powhitetrash" girls call the dignified grandmother "Annie" and mock her
in word and obscene gesture; of a grammar school graduation day robbed
of its luster by the careless hurt of a white speaker, a politician, who
promises new laboratories for the white high school and a paved sports
field for the black.

At eight she goes with her brother to live with their mother in St.
Louis. Here she is introduced to the ways of the streetwise urban blacks
with laws independent of the white dominant culture. It is a worldly rich
environment. Their gay and beautiful mother charms her children with
her singing and dancing as she charms the patrons of the bars. And she
turns the other cheek to no one. Her gang of fierce brothers holds a
covenant of loyalty as strong as that of the church brethren of Arkansas
but utterly different in its rules of reciprocity. The children at this stage belong to neither world but live in awe of their mother, never secure that she
will be really theirs forever. And Maya, at age eight, is first fondled then
raped by her mother's boyfriend. In the court of white justice he is found
guilty, given a year's sentence, and allowed to go free the same night of the
trial. In the other court of the black streets the retribution is more terrible.
He is kicked to death.

Maya and Bailey return to Stamps. She suffers guilt for having caused the man's death and the separation of her brother from the mother he adores. For a year she retreats to silence, one of the most terrible of the "Silences" that women writers have described.

That she emerged from this silence Angelou attributes to the strength of Momma, who finds her a sympathetic adult friend and who later bravely takes the children to California to their mother's guardianship, and, far beyond Momma, to her mother, Vivian Baxter, a force undaunted by sexual or racial prejudice: "To describe my mother would be to write about a hurricane in its perfect power" (58). It is strength imparted with a little tenderness; it is strength to endure hurts, not a strength that can protect her from them. The strengths and weaknesses of the family and the relationship of the girl to her family are the most important topics of discussion about the book, to which we will return.

Reunited with her mother in San Francisco, Maya lives for the first time in a home with a father provider, Daddy Clidell. She listens admiringly to the tales of con men who gather in their home, tales of duping bigoted whites rendered helpless by their very racial prejudice. Though the adult author writes with proud identification with this group, the reader does not imagine the tall, gawky teenage girl as feeling at home among them. Rather it is the story of a girl lonely at the white high school she attends, lonelier still at home.

The last year the book recounts is tumultuous. Maya spends a summer with her father and his new girlfriend and feels close to neither. On a day trip to Mexico with her father she sees him relax in a Mexican bar, a great man, tall, handsome, funny, admired by an easy crowd, and imagines the man he might have been in another culture. She drives him back dead drunk, she who had never driven a car, in a feat of success born of desperation and courage. Then after a fight with the father's girlfriend, she is dumped at someone else's house, and wanders off to sleep in a junkyard of abandoned cars and to awake to find herself in a community of homeless, runaway children. It is an odd setting for Eden but an idyll of the Golden Age nonetheless. Under the benign rule of a tall boy, "Bootsie," there was "no stealing"; "everyone worked at something," collecting bottles, mowing lawns, odd jobs. "All money was held by Bootsie and used communally" (246).

The experience has a crucial place in the work. Angelou writes:

> After a month my thinking processes had so changed that I was hardly recognizable to myself. The unquestioning acceptance by my peers had dislodged the familiar insecurity. Odd that the homeless children, the silt of

war frenzy, could initiate me into the brotherhood of man. After hunting
down unbroken bottles and selling them with a white girl from Missouri, a
Mexican girl from Los Angeles and a Black girl from Oklahoma, I was never
again to sense myself so solidly outside the pale of the human race. The lack
of criticism evidenced by our ad hoc community influenced me, and set a
tone of tolerance for my life. (247)

The brotherhood of man is a distant fellowship. With the sense of tolerance comes no closeness or love. When she returns to her mother's house,
the good-byes are simple and the welcome casual. Her oldest intimacy,
with her brother Bailey, is ruptured first by his growing identification with
"a group of slick street boys" (249), then by his leaving the house to live
with a white prostitute.

Maya lives in lonely uncertainty over approaching womanhood and
dismay over her looks. However universal the experience, it does not make
any young person feel close to others. In a desperate attempt to affirm
her sexuality, she accosts a neighbor boy. After one sexual encounter—
without feeling, without a word being spoken—she is pregnant. It is a last
mark of the isolation in which she has lived that no one notices her pregnancy until she tells her parents about it in her eighth month.

If they have not protected her, they do not desert her, but give her care
and encouragement. Maya Angelou will be a loving mother without having known tender love as a child. The book is dedicated to: "My son, Guy
Johnson and all the strong Black birds of promise who defy the odds and
gods and sing their songs."

It is our task now to see where this book fits into several literary traditions, especially a tradition of Southern literature. For background and lo-
cale, it is hard to be more Southern than Stamps, Arkansas; St. Louis is de-
batable; California is OUT. Although Maya Angelou has returned to the
South to become Z. Smith Reynolds Professor at Wake Forest University, it
is by a very circuitous route.

Her career since the close of *I Know Why the Caged Bird Sings* has made her a
citizen of the world. Her works have been among all strata of humanity.
The last of her teenage years she spent on the streets of California, where
she was a waitress, barmaid, dishwasher, nightclub entertainer, prostitute,
and madam, and where she barely escaped a life of drug addiction. From
this life she became part of a world tour of *Porgy and Bess*. She has since been
an actress, dancer, and producer of shows for Broadway and TV. She has
been a journalist and editor, poet and author of her autobiographical
books. She has lived and worked in Africa. She has served as a coordinator

for the Southern Christian Leadership Conference. She has been a university administrator and professor in Ghana, in California, in Kansas, and at Wake Forest. She holds honorary degrees from a dozen institutions.

The South that she lived in and that her kinsmen close and distant fled makes part of her past. But she has been eager to put as much distance between herself and its white bourgeois traditions in literature as in life. The only black she speaks of with real scorn in this book is the father's priggish girlfriend who apes the ways of middle-class white women. She is a "small tight woman from the South" who "kept the house clean with the orderliness of a coffin"; who "was on close terms with her washing machine and her ironing board"; who "had all the poses of the Black bourgeoisie without the material bases to support the postures" (221). With more pity but no closer identification, she recounts that the poor black girls of Stamps were marked by the trivial traditions of Southern white women: "Ridiculous and even ludicrous. But Negro girls in small Southern towns, whether poverty-stricken or just munching along on a few of life's necessities, were given as extensive and irrelevant preparations for adulthood as rich white girls shown in magazines," the irrelevancies of "mid-Victorian values" (101). With money earned picking cotton and with fingers too coarse for the work, they yet bought tatting or embroidery thread, and Maya herself had "a lifetime's supply of dainty doilies that would never be used in sacheted dresser drawers" (101).

Although in ceasing to be Marguerite Johnson of Stamps, Arkansas, and in becoming Maya Angelou the writer, she denies the traditions—for blacks or for women—of the white South, the same themes most often called Southern fill her work. None, of course, is exclusively or originally Southern, and looking at the other traditions her work pertains to makes this very clear.

Speaking of her years in Africa and her marriage to an African, Angelou said that Ghana taught her to see the survival of distinctly African ways among Afro-Americans ("The Black Scholar Interviews: Maya Angelou," 49). These affect her portrayal of character, individually and collectively. In *I Know Why the Caged Bird Sings* she describes Momma's reluctance to be questioned or to tell all she knows as her "African-bush secretiveness and suspiciousness" (189), which has been only "compounded by slavery and confirmed by centuries of promises made and promises broken" (189). She relates the habits of address—calling neighbors "Uncle," "Sister," "Cousin"—to a heritage of tribal belonging.

As a writer she says she works from her ear, from listening to her people's cadences and habits of speech. Here she is like other Southern writers, such as Faulkner, Welty, O'Connor, Lee Smith, whose works capture the language as spoken in particular places by particular people; she differs from them in her insistence on the uniqueness of black language as the means of black survival and of triumph: "It may be enough, however, to have it said that we survive in exact relationship to the dedication of our poets (include preachers, musicians and blues singers)" (180). But she nowhere limits herself to the tongues of black Arkansas or ghetto streets. One critic has praised her "avoidance of a monolithic Black language" (O'Neale, 34) and the fact that she "does not overburden black communicants with clumsy versions of homespun black speech" (O'Neale, 35). In the white high school she attended in San Francisco, Angelou became conscious that she would use two languages: "We learned to slide out of one language and into another without being conscious of the effort. At school, in a given situation, we might respond with 'That's not unusual.' But in the street, meeting the same situation, we easily said, 'It be's like that sometimes'" (219). I have said that the point of view of the book goes back and forth between that of the inexperienced girl and the experienced writer. The language also moves between a strong, colloquial simplicity and a sometimes overblown literary mannerism. Though she does not overuse black folk speech, she never errs when she uses it as she does in such literary passages as this one, describing her self-pride on graduation day: "Youth and social approval allied themselves with me and we trammeled memories of slights and insults. The wind of our swift passage remodeled my features. Lost tears were pounded to the mud and then to dust. Years of withdrawal were brushed aside and left behind, as hanging ropes of parasitic moss" (167). (Whether this is more embarrassing to Southern literature than the false inflections of Southern accents offered us by Hollywood or TV is for you to judge!)

The literary traditions not often allied to Southern literature that undergird this work are those of a long Western tradition of the *bildungsroman*— a novel, often autobiographical, of a young person's growing up and finding his way among the traditions and values of the family and culture in which he or she is reared—and a long tradition in this country of Afro-American autobiography. In a sense both come together in this book; some critics have referred to it interchangeably as novel and autobiography. But the traditions are diametrically opposite in the ways the hero or heroine is portrayed.

In the *bildungsroman* the loneliness of the hero is expected. Youth is self-conscious; the hero feels that the values of his family and culture are oppressive to him; he must make his escape. It is an international genre including Goethe's *Wilhelm Meister* and James Joyce's *A Portrait of the Artist as a Young Man*, with outstanding examples in Southern literature, including Thomas Wolfe's *Look Homeward, Angel* and Richard Wright's *Native Son*. It influences women's works like Kate Chopin's *The Awakening*, and, with the publication of this first of Angelou's works in 1970 and a host of other important books that appeared in the same decade, it affects a vital new tradition in black women's writings.

Before the publication in 1940 of Wright's *Native Son*, fiction by American black writers constituted a smaller and less important body of work than the long tradition of Afro-American autobiographies arising from the narratives of escaped or redeemed slaves. In these autobiographies, the primary mode of black American prose, the role of the hero is altogether different; he is not a lonely misfit, not a rejector of his people but their exemplum. One critic, Selwyn R. Cudjoe, says that the authority of these writings derives from the impersonality of the hero-narrator:

> [T]he Afro-American autobiographical statement as a form tends to be bereft of any excessive subjectivism and mindless egotism. Instead, it presents the Afro-American as reflecting a much more *im-personal* condition, the autobiographical subject emerging as an almost random member of the group, selected to tell his/her tale. As a consequence, the Afro-American autobiographical statement emerges as a *public* rather than a *private* gesture, *me-ism* gives way to *our-ism* and superficial concerns about *individual subject* usually give way to the collective subjection of the group. The autobiography, therefore, is objective and realistic in its approach and is presumed generally to be of service to the group. (Cudjoe, 9-10)

Cudjoe lumps together autobiography and fiction: "Autobiography and fiction, then, are simply different means of arriving at or (re)cognizing the same truth: the reality of American life and the position of the Afro-American subject in that life. Neither genre should be given a privileged position in our literary history and each should be judged on its ability to speak honestly and perceptively about Black experience in this land" (Cudjoe, 8).

Asked this question, "Do you consider your quartet to be autobiographical novels or autobiographies?" Angelou replied, "They are autobiographies," and she went on to define her intent there as reporting on a collective, not a lone individual's story. "When I wrote *I Know Why the Caged Bird Sings*, I wasn't thinking so much about my own life or identity. I was thinking about a particular time in which I lived and the influences of that time on a number of people. I kept thinking, what about that time? What were the people around young Maya doing? I used the central figure—

myself—as a focus to show how one person can make it through those times" ("Interview with Claudia Tate," 6).

Whether we call the work "fiction" or "autobiography" *does* really matter more than just giving English teachers something to argue about. Different traditions affect the stance of the writer to her work and the responses of the reader. Especially on the most important questions of debate about this work, the nature of the family or group she portrays and the nature of the relationship of the central character to that group, the two traditions we have looked at pose different solutions. In a *bildungsroman*—or apprenticeship novel—we expect detachment from or rejection of the group mores. In the tradition of black autobiography here described we expect total or unconscious absorption in the group. The role of the black woman in this tradition has been called that of "an all-pervading absence" (Cudjoe, 7). Few of many thousand such autobiographies written were by or about women. In those written by men they play a distinctly subservient role: "they never really seemed to have lived worthy of emulation. They invariably seemed to live for others, for Black men or White; for children, or for parents; bereft, always it appeared, of an autonomous self" (Cudjoe, 11).

Two important breaks in tradition have come in the twentieth century. In 1945 Richard Wright published his autobiography, *Black Boy,* and touched off a debate that has not ended about the nature of the black experience in America. His hero is not a random member of a group who are victims of white oppression. The white oppressors are there, but the boy suffers as much from his black family members, who have become, under the heritage of slavery, subhuman in their hunger, fear, ignorance, superstition, brutality, and despair. By the miracle of books he is awakened to a life none of his family could comprehend. Years later, as a grown man, he saw the father who laughed at his hunger, saw him as a peasant of the soil and as an animal: "how chained were his actions and emotions to the direct, animalistic impulses of his withering body" (Wright, 43). The mature Wright pitied and forgave his father, but he retained the lesson that he had to distance himself from his family or perish. Black writers especially have argued against his assertions:

> After I had outlived the shocks of childhood, after the habit of reflection had been born in me, I used to mull over the strange absence of real kindness in Negroes, how unstable was our tenderness, how lacking in genuine passion we were, how void of great hope, how timid our joy, how bare our

traditions, how hollow our memories, how lacking we were in those intangible sentiments that bind man to man, and how shallow was even our despair. (Wright, 45)

Much in *I Know Why the Caged Bird Sings* and in what Angelou has said about her writing shows her in opposition to Wright's dogma. Though the girl is lonely and hurt, she finds her way to survival in terms of the traditions of her family, her mother and her grandmother, not in opposition to them. She does remark that she knew few expressions of tenderness. The grandmother was embarrassed to discuss any emotions not associated with her religious faith; the mother imparts power but not tenderness. She describes her: "Vivian Baxter had no mercy. There was a saying in Oakland at the time which, if she didn't say it herself, explained her attitude. The saying was, 'Sympathy is next to shit in the dictionary, and I can't even read.' . . . She had the impartiality of nature, with the same lack of indulgence or clemency" (201–02). In stressing her discovery of continuance of African ways among American blacks, she argues with Wright's judgment that black traditions were "bare." In her description of her use of the mode of autobiography, she says she was writing of one who typifies, not one who opposes or escapes the group.

I Know Why the Caged Bird Sings appeared in 1970. In the same year appeared Toni Morrison's *The Bluest Eye,* Alice Walker's *The Third Life of Grange Copeland,* Louise Meriwether's *Daddy Was a Numbers Runner,* Michele Wallace's *Black Macho and the Myth of the Superwoman,* and Nikki Giovanni's *Black Feeling, Black Talk/Black Judgement.* In these and other notable works of the 1970s— including Ntozake Shange's *For Colored Girls Who Have Considered Suicide/When the Rainbow Is Enuf* (Broadway, 1976)—black women writers have debated the effects of black sexism, and many have asserted that they must find their identity not merely in opposition to the traditions for the woman that the black culture imposes.

Angelou has put herself apart consistently from the movement of white women's liberation. Black women, she says, have never been as subservient within their community as white women in theirs: "White men, who are in effect their fathers, husbands, brothers, their sons, nephews and uncles, say to white women, or imply in any case: 'I don't really need you to run my institutions. I need you in certain places and in those places you must be kept—in the bedroom, in the kitchen, in the nursery, and on the pedestal.' Black women have never been told this" ("Interview with Claudia Tate," 3). Though they have not occupied the pulpits, black women have been leaders in their communities, according to Angelou. She is pleased with the dialogue that these black women's works have begun. Though she has been criticized for including the rape in *I Know Why the Caged Bird Sings,* she says the whole truth must be told, and she says there is much truth still to be told about the male point of view of such works as *For Colored Girls Who Have Considered Suicide.*

Angelou's works and words point to her conviction that the black tradition is adequate and good, that black women emerge from it triumphant and strong. Critics have noted the absence of significant men in her autobiographies, and she certainly has been, since her years of teenage motherhood, a woman who had to survive on her own strengths. In the midst of the debate of the 1970s over the place of women in black culture, she affirmed that, subservient to no one, she was willing and honored to "serve." As one who had to work to survive, she says she has always been "liberated":

> I am so "liberated" that except on rare occasions my husband does not walk into the house without seeing his dinner prepared. He does not have to concern himself about a dirty house, I do that, for myself but also for my husband. I think it is important to make that very clear.
>
> I think there is something gracious and graceful about serving. Now, unfortunately, or rather the truth is, our history in this country has been the history of the servers and because we were forced to serve and because dignity was absolutely drained from the servant, for anyone who serves in this country, black or white, is looked upon with such revilement, they are held in such contempt while that is not true in other parts of the world. In Africa it is a great honor to serve. ("The Black Scholar Interviews: Maya Angelou," 47)

I Know Why the Caged Bird Sings is sixteen years old now, the experience it recounts more than forty years old. Yet nothing, it seems, could be more timely.

It is an admirable story; and it is not typical. Typically the black girl who has no permanent father in her home; who is shuffled between mother and grandmother, city and country; who is raped at eight, a mother at sixteen; who supports her child, without help from its father or from her own mother, with odd jobs, waitressing, bartending, prostitution— typically such girls do not become *Ladies Home Journal's* Woman of the Year for Communications or Z. Smith Reynolds Professor at Wake Forest University or recipients of a dozen honorary degrees. For all Angelou's heroic assertion that the black woman emerges victorious from oppression and abuse, most of them do not. They are not equipped to succeed by any of the traditions here laid out—not that of the dominant white bourgeoisie, which taught a generation of Southern women, black and white, to sew and crochet and be debutantes; not that of the pious black churchwomen who look for reward and vindication in the next life; not that of the black streets where one of her mother's boyfriends was kicked to death and another one shot and where Angelou once herself took a pistol to the home of a boy who had threatened her son. Few black women have had work so well for them the swift vengeance outside the law; they have been victims of lawlessness as cruel as the law that first held them oppressed and then neglected their victimization.

Angelou knows it is a heroic, not a typical, model. The dedication, you remember, is to her son and to "all the strong Black birds of promise who defy the odds and gods."

One last note. Bearing the emphasis on family with tradition we have seen common to Southern literature, this book bears no mark of the provincialism of which not only Southern literature but much of American literature of recent decades, especially the literature of American women, has been accused.

Non-American writers such as Salman Rushdie and Nadine Gordimer complained loudly that ours has become a literature of the misunderstood individual. It abounds in complaints and self-centered preoccupations (will the heroine, like Gail Godwin's Odd Woman, achieve orgasm); it finds little room for the hunger of the children of the world or for the brutalities of police states.

Artistically Maya Angelou may err on the side of didacticism, but she is free of exaggerated self-concern. The voice in the story shifts from the girl of limited experience and perspective to that of the writer who speaks with the authority of truths gleaned from traditions as diverse as Shakespeare and Ghanian folk tale. By her work she has not only contributed to but also expanded the American literary tradition and the perspective from which this literature views—and serves—the world.

Works Cited

Angelou, Maya. *I Know Why the Caged Bird Sings* (New York: Random House, 1969).

———. "The Black Scholar Interviews: Maya Angelou." *The Black Scholar* 8, no. 4, (Jan.–Feb. 1977): 44–53.

———. "Interview with Claudia Tate," in *Black Women Writers at Work*. Ed. Claudia Tate (New York: Continuum, 1983).

Cudjoe, Selwyn R. "Maya Angelou and the Autobiographical Statement," in *Black Women Writers (1950–1980)*. Ed. Mari Evans (New York: Anchor Press/Doubleday, 1983), 6–24.

Goodman, George. "Maya Angelou's Lonely Black Outlook." *New York Times.* Mar. 24, 1972.

Gross, Robert A. "Growing Up Black." *Newsweek.* Mar. 2, 1970, 89–90.

Harris, Joan K. "The Kindness of Strangers." *Times Educational Supplement*, Oct. 19, 1984, 48.

Kelly, Ernece B., Review "I Know Why the Caged Bird Sings." *Harvard Educational Review* 40 (Nov. 1970): 681–82.

Kent, George E. "Maya Angelou's *I Know Why the Caged Bird Sings* and Black Autobiographical Tradition." *Kansas Quarterly* 3 (1975).

Lehmann-Haupt, Christopher. "Masculine and Feminine" (Review of *Sugar Ray* by Sugar Ray Robinson and of *I Know Why the Caged Bird Sings*). *New York Times.* Feb. 25, 1970.

O'Neale, Sondra. "Reconstruction of the Composite Self: New Images of Black Women in Maya Angelou's Continuing Autobiography," in *Black Women Writers (1950–1980)*. Ed. Mari Evans (New York: Anchor Press/ Doubleday, 1983), 25–36.

Smith, Sidonie Ann. "The Song of a Caged Bird: Quest after Self-Acceptance." *Southern Humanities Review* 8 (Fall 1973): 365–75.

Wright, Richard. *Black Boy: A Record of Childhood and Youth.* New York: Perennial Classics, 1966.

Death as Metaphor of Self

LILIANE K. ARENSBERG

◆　◆　◆

When I think about myself,
I almost laugh myself to death,
My life has been one great big joke,
A dance that's walked
A song that's spoke
I laugh so hard I almost choke
When I think about myself.
———Maya Angelou

IN 1970, AT A TIME when most blacks and a growing number of lib-
eral whites affirmed the ad-campaign motto that "Black Is Beautiful,"
Maya Angelou's autobiography was published. An unbeautiful, awkward,
rather morose, dreamy, and "too-big Negro girl," young Maya Angelou
seems an unlikely heroine. Neither the pretty and radiant prom queen of
her all-black high school, like Anne Moody in *Coming of Age in Mississippi,*
nor the acknowledged genius of her doting family like Nikki Giovanni in
Gemini, the child Angelou writes about is unadmired, unenvied, uncoddled
as she makes her precarious way (on "broad feet," she reminds us) into the
world.

Spanning the first sixteen years of her life, *I Know Why the Caged Bird Sings*
opens with Maya Angelou's[1] arrival, at the green age of three, in dusty
Stamps, Arkansas. Her parents' marriage dissolved, Maya and her older
brother, Bailey, have been sent across country from their parents' home in
Long Beach, California, to Momma's, their paternal grandmother's, in
Stamps. After five years of chores, books, fantasies, and escapades with Bailey, Maya rejoins her mother in teeming, gray St. Louis. There she is raped,
at age eight, by her mother's lover, who in retaliation is murdered by her
uncles. A guilt-ridden, terrified, and bewildered "woman," Maya is again

111

sent to Stamps. Upon her graduation from Lafayette County Training School, at age fourteen Maya rejoins her mother, now living in San Francisco. She spends part of one summer at a trailer camp in Southern California with her father and his lover, Dolores. After returning with him from a jaunt into Mexico, Maya is stabbed in a quarrel with Dolores. Fearing another murderous reprisal, Maya is unwilling to return to any of her homes. Instead, she seeks refuge in a car junkyard. There "a collage of Negro, Mexican and white" youths initiate her into a redeeming vision of universal brotherhood—one that Malcolm X could only discover thousands of miles from the United States in Mecca. She returns to San Francisco, a sobered and self-possessed young woman, and challenges the racial bar to be hired as the town's first black female streetcar conductor. At the end of the book Maya becomes mother to an illegitimate son, the offspring of her "immaculate pregnancy."

This brief sketch, though excluding some very crucial personalities and episodes in her youth, emphasizes the rootlessness of Maya Angelou's early years. Angelou herself underscores this pattern of mobility in the opening phrase of her introduction:

"What are you looking at me for?
I didn't come to stay. . . ."[2]

Indeed, geographic movement and temporary residence become formative aspects of her growing identity—equal in importance to experiences and relationships more commonly regarded as instrumental in forming the adult self. Appropriately, this poetic phrase becomes the young girl's motto, or "shield" (58) as Angelou calls it, Maya's means of proclaiming her isolation while defending against its infringement.

Shuttled between temporary homes and transient allegiances, Maya necessarily develops a stoic flexibility that becomes not only her "shield," but, more important, her characteristic means of dealing with the world. This flexibility is both blessing and curse: it enables her to adapt to various and changing environments, but it also keeps her forever threatened with loss or breakdown of her identity, as will presently be shown.

Indeed, Angelou's descriptions of her younger self seem almost entirely composed of negatives: she is not wanted by her parents, who hold over her the unspoken but everpresent threat of banishment; she is not beautiful or articulate like her brother, Bailey; she is too introverted and passive to assert herself on her environment; and, finally, she is a child in a world of enigmatic adults, and a black girl in a world created by and for the benefit of white men.

Furthermore, Maya's geographic worlds are each separate and self-contained. There is the world of Momma and her store in Stamps, a puritan world of racial pride, religious devotion, and acquiescence to one's worldly lot. And there is her "wild and beautiful" mother's world of pool halls, card sharks, fast dancing, fast talking, and fast loving. Combining and transcending both is the private and portable world of Maya's imagination.

If there is one stable element in Angelou's youth it is this dependence on books. Kipling, Poe, Austen, and Thackeray, Dunbar, Johnson, Hughes, and Du Bois, *The Lone Ranger, The Shadow,* and Captain Marvel comics—all are equally precious to this lonely girl. Shakespeare, whose Sonnet 29 speaks to Maya's own social and emotional alienation, becomes her "first white love" (11). As it does for Mary Antin, Anaïs Nin, and other female autobiographers, the public library becomes a quiet refuge from the chaos of her personal life. "I took out my first library card in St. Louis" (64), she notes. And it is the public library she attempts to reach after her rape. Later, when running away from her father, she hides in a library. Indeed, when her life is in crisis, Maya characteristically escapes into the world of books.

As artifacts creating complete and meaningful universes, novels and their heroes become means by which Maya apprehends and judges her own bewildering world. Thus, Louise, her first girlfriend, reminds Maya of Jane Eyre; Louise's mother, a domestic, Maya refers to as a governess. Mrs. Flowers, who introduces her to the magic of books, appeals to Maya because she was like "women in English novels who walked the moors . . . with their loyal dogs racing at a respectful distance. Like the women who sat in front of roaring fireplaces, drinking tea incessantly from silver trays full of scones and crumpets. Women who walked the 'heath' and read morocco-bound books and had two last names divided by a hyphen." Curiously, it is this imaginative association with a distant, extinct, and colonial world that makes Mrs. Flowers one who "made me proud to be Negro, just by being herself" (79).

But the plight of lovers, madmen and poets is also Maya's problem. "The little princesses who were mistaken for maids, and the long-lost children mistaken for waifs," writes Angelou, "became more real to me than our house, our mother, our school or Mr. Freeman" (64). She is so consummately involved in the world of fantasy that even while being raped she "was sure any minute my mother or Bailey or the Green Hornet would burst in the door and save me" (65).

As in this quotation, the style by which Angelou describes her youth seems in counterpoint to the meaning of her narrative. It is written with a humor and wry wit that belies the personal and racial tragedies recorded. Since style is such a revealing element in all autobiographies, hers, especially, seems a conscious defense against the pain felt at evoking unpleasant memories. Moreover, wit operates as a formidable tool of the outraged adult; by mocking her enemies, Angelou overcomes them. Thus the gluttonous Reverend Thomas gets his just desserts at church when, "throwing out phrases like home-run balls," he loses his dentures in a scuffle with an overzealous parishioner; the self-serving condescension of "fluttering" Mrs. Cullinan is ridiculed in a "tragic ballad" on "being white, fat, old and without children" (so, too, with the vanity and carelessness of her mother's "lipstick kisses" and her father's pompous *"ers* and *errers"* as he struts among Stamps's curious "down-home folk"). The adult writer's irony retaliates for the tongue-tied child's helpless pain.

The primary object, however, for Angelou's wit is herself. At times maudlin, always highly romantic and withdrawn, the young Maya is a person the older writer continually finds comic. Her idolatrous attachment to Bailey, her projections of fantasy upon reality, her reverence for her mother's stunning beauty, her strained attempts at sympathy for her self-enamoured father, her ingenuous attitude towards sexuality—these are but a few of the many and recurring aspects of her younger self the adult mocks.

The basic motive for writing one's autobiography, some believe, is to be understood, accepted, and loved. Angelou's willingness to ridicule former self-deceptions—more precisely, her former self—indicates the adult's fearlessness of the reader's judgments and her own critical stance toward herself. If Angelou's voice in re-creating her past is, therefore, ironic, it is however supremely controlled.

Nevertheless, despite the frankness of her narrative, Angelou avoids charting a direct path to her present self. Unlike *Gemini* or *Coming of Age in Mississippi* or *The Autobiography of Malcolm X* or Richard Wright's *Black Boy*— books in the same genre—Angelou's autobiography barely mentions the emergent woman within the girlish actor. Although Roy Pascal believes that "the autobiographer must refer us continually outwards and onwards, to the author himself and to the outcome of all the experiences,"[3] Maya Angelou proves an exception to the rule.

Because Angelou's apprehension of experience and, indeed, herself, is essentially protean and existential, it is difficult to find one overriding identity of the adult self controlling her narrative. For what connects the adult and the child is less a linear development toward one distinct version of the self through career or philosophy than an ever-changing multiplicity of

possibilities. It is, in fact, her mutability, born of and affirmed through re-
peated movement, reorientation and assimilation, that becomes Angelou's
unique identity, her "identity theme,"[4] to use Heinz Lichtenstein's more
precise term. And if "work, in man, serves the maintenance of the individual's identity theme,"[5] as Lichtenstein asserts, then the numerous
careers of the adult Angelou—as dancer, prostitute, S.C.L.C. organizer,
actor, poet, journalist, and director—document her restlessness and
resilience.

The unsettled life Angelou writes about in *I Know Why the Caged Bird Sings*
suggests a sense of self as perpetually in the process of becoming, of dying
and being reborn, in all its ramifications. Thus death (and to some extent
its companion concept, rebirth) is the term by which her "identity theme"
operates. It is the metaphor of self that most directly and comprehensively
communicates Angelou's identity. Moreover, the compulsion to repeat—
a necessary instrument for the maintenance of any "identity theme"[6]—
adds credence to the power of this major motif in Angelou's narrative. For,
while the book's tone is predominantly witty, even light, resonating just
below the surface of almost every page of Angelou's autobiography is the
hidden, but everpresent, theme of death.

Angelou introduces *I Know Why the Caged Bird Sings* with an anecdote. It is
Easter Sunday at the Colored Methodist Episcopal Church in Stamps. In
celebration of the event, Momma has prepared a lavender taffeta dress for
Maya. Believing it to be the most beautiful dress she has ever seen, Maya attributes to it magical properties: when worn, the dress will change Maya
into the lovely, blond, and blue-eyed "sweet little white girl" she actually
believes herself to be.

But on Easter morning the dress reveals its depressing actuality: it is "a
plain, ugly cut-down from a white woman's once-was-purple throwaway."
No Cinderella metamorphosis for Maya; instead, she lives in a "black
dream" from which there is no respite. Unlike Christ, whose resurrection
from death the church is celebrating, Maya cannot be reborn into another
life. Overcome with the impossibility of her white fantasy, she escapes the
church "peeing and crying" her way home. Maya must, indeed, lose control of her body and feelings. "It would probably run right back up to my
head," she believes, "and my poor head would burst like a dropped water-
melon, and all the brains and spit and tongue and eyes would roll all over
the place" (3). By letting go of her fantasy—physically manifested by letting go of her bladder—Maya will not "die from a busted head."

But, to "let go," as Erik Erikson observes in *Childhood and Society*, "can
turn into an inimical letting loose of destructive forces."[7] For, on this

Easter Sunday Maya Angelou comprehends the futility of her wish to become "one of the sweet little white girls who were everybody's dream of what was right with the world." "If growing up is painful for the Southern Black girl," the adult writer concludes, "being aware of her displacement is the rust on the razor that threatens the throat." Although she acknowledges the "unnecessary insult" of her own white fantasy, Angelou nevertheless puts the rust on the razor by her awareness of its insidious and ubiquitous presence.[8]

The form an autobiography takes is as revealing as its style and content. By placing this anecdote before the body of her narrative, Angelou asserts the paradigmatic importance of this particular event on her life. The atemporality of this experience (Maya's age remains unmentioned) coupled with the symbolic setting of Easter Sunday, suggests a personal myth deeply embedded in Angelou's unconscious. One could, indeed, speculate that this event, introducing Maya Angelou's autobiography, is the "epiphanic moment" of her youth. For this short narrative presents the two dynamic operatives that circumscribe Angelou's self: her blackness and her outcast position.

Immediately striking in the anecdote is Maya's fantastic belief that "I was really white," that "a cruel fairy stepmother, who was understandably jealous of my beauty" (2) had tricked Maya of her Caucasian birthright. The fairy tale imagery employed to depict her creation is characteristic of the imaginative and impressionable girl, but the meaning of her tale cannot be overlooked. For, according to her schema, Maya's identity hinges on the whims of this fairy stepmother. If benevolent, she will transform Maya back into a pretty white girl; if she remains cruel, her spell over Maya will rest unbroken. When her dress does not produce the longed-for results, Maya is forced to contend with her blackness. But if she acknowledges this blackness, Maya must also acknowledge the existence of an arbitrary and malevolent force beyond her control that dictates her personal and racial identity.

As if mourning the death of the lovely white body beyond her possession, Maya describes her dress as sounding "like crepe paper on the back of hearses" (1). Maya's body indeed becomes a symbolic hearse, containing not only her dead dream but also a life whose very existence is threatened by the whims of a murderous white culture.

Angelou's highly personal confession of racial self-hatred is, unfortunately, not unique in Afro-American experience. Many works of contemporary black novelists and autobiographers—from Ralph Ellison and Imamu Baraka/LeRoi Jones to Richard Wright and Malcolm X—assert that invisibility, violence, alienation, and death are part and parcel of growing up black in a white America. Likewise, psychological and sociological studies affirm that the first lesson in living taught the black child is how to ensure his or her survival. "The child must know," write Grier and Cobbs, "that the white world is dangerous and that if he does not understand its rules it may kill him."⁹ It is, then, pitifully understandable for Maya to wish herself white, since blackness forebodes annihilation.

Of equal significance in this introductory anecdote is Maya's belief that a stepmother has put her under this spell and then abandoned her. Her image of herself, for at least the first five years of life, is that of an orphan. Even later, when forced to recognize the existence of both her parents, she still clings to this orphan identity. Although acknowledging that Bailey, by dint of beauty and personality, is his parents' true son, she describes herself as "an orphan that they had picked up to provide Bailey with company" (45).

While her father is as culpable as her mother in Maya's abandonment, it is nevertheless her mother whom Maya most yearns for and consequently blames. No real mother would "laugh and eat oranges in the sunshine without her children" (42), Maya reflects bitterly when first confronted with her mother's existence. No proper mother should let her child so profoundly mourn her passing as Maya has done.

> I could cry anytime I wanted by picturing my mother (I didn't know what she looked like) lying in her coffin. Her hair, which was black, was spread out on a tiny little pillow and her body was covered with a sheet. The face was brown, like a big O, and since I couldn't fill in the features I printed M O T H E R across the O, and tears would fall down my cheeks like warm milk. (43)

Maya's image of her dead mother is deeply comforting to the child. The protective and nurturing maternal love Maya yearns for is symbolically created through her own tears: they "would fall down my cheeks like warm milk." Consider then, the shock, the affront to her tottering self-image as well as to the image of her dead mother, when Maya receives her mother's first Christmas presents. Not only is her mother alive, but Maya herself must have been as good as dead during those early years of separation.

Adding insult to injury are the " awful presents" themselves: "a tea set—a teapot, four cups and saucers and tiny spoons—and a doll with blue eyes and rosy cheeks and yellow hair painted on her head" (43). Symbols of a white world beyond Maya's reach or everyday experience, these toys not only evidence her mother's exotic and alien life but also intimate questions of guilt and banishment no five-year-old can answer. The doll, especially, whose description so closely parallels Maya's own wished-for physical appearance, is an intolerable presence. It serves as an effigy of her mother by virtue of being female and her gift, as well as of Maya's impossible fantasy; Maya and Bailey "tore the stuffing out of the doll the day after Christmas" (44).

Abandonment by a dead mother is forgivable, but abandonment by a living one evokes a rage so threatening that it must undergo massive repression. Thus, Maya becomes passive, inhibiting her deep anger and hostility. The fear of abandonment, even when living with her mother in St. Louis, never abates. "If we got on her nerves or if we were disobedient, she could always send us back to Stamps. The weight of appreciation and the threat, which was never spoken, of a return to Momma were burdens that clogged my childish wits into impassivity. I was called Old Lady and chided for moving and talking like winter's molasses" (57). Maya's fears come true; after her rape she is again banished to Stamps.

Nevertheles, Maya repeatedly protests fondness for her mother. Beautiful, honest, gay, and tough, Vivian Baxter leaves her daughter awestruck. "I could never put my finger on her realness," Angelou writes. "She was so pretty and so quick that . . . I thought she looked like the Virgin Mary" (57). So much is Vivian Baxter idealized that Angelou capitalizes "Mother" in her narrative, while "father" remains in lowercase. But Vivian Baxter is diametrically opposite to the brown-faced nurturing mother Maya had mourned and yearned for in Stamps. Her beauty and animation keep Maya suspicious of their consanguinity.

Maya's ambivalence about her mother—her fear and love, her rage and need for her, her isolation and her desire for closeness—is never fully resolved. Although she insists verbally on this love, her affect reveals sullenness, resignation, depression, and overwhelming passivity. Maya's aggression against her mother is well-defended, and thus specific suggestions of hostility toward her are rare. But the proliferating references to death in Angelou's autobiography provide another route for releasing Maya's (and Angelou's) repressed violent aggression.

This aspect of death's overdetermined significance is important but by no means the only level of reference; at least five subthemes, each bearing on the major theme of death, emerge in *I Know Why the Caged Bird Sings*. The first is the most obvious: the realistic fear of whites that Momma and the Southern black community have drummed into Maya. Momma, Angelou writes, "didn't cotton to the idea that white folks could be talked to at all without risking one's life" (39). The white lynchers whom Uncle Willie hides from in the vegetable bin, the taunting "powhitetrash" girls, the bloated dead man fished out of the river—all are daily proof of a predatory white world. This fact leads Angelou to a bitter conclusion: "the Black woman in the South who raises sons, grandsons and nephews had her heartstrings tied to a hanging noose" (95).

The daily fear of murder at the hands of whites leads the Southern black community into the haven of religion and the belief of a blessed reward in "the far off bye and bye." Thus, Southern black religion celebrates death, since life itself is too precarious to pin one's hopes on. Even at the revival meeting attended by members from a variety of Southern churches, death continually asserts its presence: the cardboard fans flourished by the worshippers advertise Texarkana's largest Negro funeral parlor. "People whose history and future were threatened each day by extinction," comments Angelou, "considered that it was only by divine intervention that they were able to live at all" (101).

Balancing this image of a white world threatening her own and her people's lives is Maya's revenge fantasy of murdering the offending whites. When Dentist Lincoln refuses to treat her toothache, Maya creates an elaborate reverie wherein a Herculean Momma has the cowering dentist pleading for his life: "Yes, ma'am. Thank you for not killing me. Thank you, Mrs. Henderson" (162).

Far and away the most dramatic instance of this revenge theme occurs the day of Maya's graduation from Lafayette County Training School. Unable to stand the invited white speaker's "dead words," which systematically destroy the dreams and aspirations of the black children and their elders, Maya wills them all dead:

> Then I wished that Gabriel Prosser and Nat Turner had killed all white-folks in their beds and that Abraham Lincoln had been assassinated before the signing of the Emancipation Proclamation, and that Harriet Tubman had been killed by that blow on her head and Christopher Columbus had drowned in the *Santa Maria*.
>
> It was awful to be Negro and have no control over my life. It was brutal to be young and already trained to sit quietly and listen to charges brought against my color with no chance of defense. We should all be dead. I thought I should like to see us all dead, one on top of the other. A pyramid of flesh with the whitefolks on the bottom, as the broad base, then the Indians with their silly tomahawks and teepees and wigwams and treaties, the Negroes with their mops and recipes and cotton sacks and spirituals sticking

out of their mouths. The Dutch children should all stumble in their wooden shoes and break their necks. The French should choke to death on the Louisiana Purchase (1803) while silkworms ate all the Chinese with their stupid pigtails. As a species, we were an abomination. All of us. (152–53)

Operating on a more personal level is the violence Maya witnesses within the members of her own family. Angelou introduces her Uncle Willie by describing his method of pushing her and Bailey onto the Store's red heater if they neglect their lessons. Momma, too, does not spare the rod when she believes her grandchildren remiss in hygiene, schooling, manners, or piety. But this corporal punishment—executed more in love than in rage—is small matter, indeed, when compared to the fundamental brutality of Maya's maternal relations in St. Louis. Her maternal grandfather and uncles revel in their own "meanness": "They beat up whites and Blacks with the same abandon" (56). Even her mother is not immune from her family's violent streak. Once, in retaliation for being cursed, Vivian Baxter, with the aid of her brothers, "crashed the man's head with a policemen's billy enough to leave him just this side of death" (55). Later Vivian Baxter, again in response to an insult, shoots the partner of her gambling casino.

As the climax of this familial violence, Mr. Freeman's rape is performed under the threat of death: "If you scream, I'm gonna kill you. And if you tell, I'm gonna kill Bailey" (65). But her family's response to Maya's subsequent withdrawal into silent passivity is itself another form of violence: "For a while I was punished for being so uppity that I wouldn't speak; and then came the thrashings, given by any relative who felt himself offended" (73). The rape itself is the most flagrant example of her maternal family's characteristic combination of aggression and neglect. Not only is Mr. Freeman her mother's lover, but mother and children all live under his roof. Ruthless in her quest for material comfort, Vivian Baxter is not above taking full advantage of Freeman's obvious adoration. Already at eight a sagacious observer, Maya responds with mixed emotions to her mother's relationship with Freeman. "I felt sorry for Mr. Freeman. I felt as sorry for him as I had felt for a litter of helpless pigs born in our backyard sty in Arkansas. We fattened the pigs all year long for the slaughter on the first good frost, and even as I suffered for the cute little wiggly things, I knew how much I was going to enjoy the fresh sausage and hog's headcheese they could give me only with their deaths" (60).

Of course, Maya's sympathy for Freeman has another cause: she feels as neglected by Vivian Baxter as he does. And while Freeman's motives in the earlier masturbatory episodes and even the rape itself probably stem as much from revenge against the mother as easy access to the daughter, Maya's own need for attention and physical closeness cannot be overlooked. After the first of these episodes, Angelou writes, "came the nice part. He held me so softly that I wished he wouldn't ever let me go. I felt at home. From the way he was holding me I knew he'd never let me go or let anything bad ever happen to me. This was probably my real father and we had found each other at last" (61). Pitifully unable to distinguish lust from paternal love (never having experienced the latter), Maya projects onto Freeman this physical warmth missing from all her relationships with adults. "I began to feel lonely for Mr. Freeman and the encasement of his big arms," Angelou recalls. "Before, my world had been Bailey, food, Momma, the Store, reading books and Uncle Willie. Now, for the first time, it included physical contact" (62).

Freeman's subsequent murder (he was kicked to death by her uncles) evokes overwhelming guilt in Maya. At Freeman's trial Maya gives false testimony about their encounters, and now "a man was dead because I lied" (72). Associating her spoken word with death, Maya stops talking.

Maya as bearer of death is the fourth dimension of death and violence in Angelou's narrative. In disgrace with God because "I had sold myself to the Devil and there could be no escape," Maya conceives herself to be the cursed instrument of violent death. This conviction is part of the pattern of self-rejection and inferiority well-established within Maya's psyche; it lies but one small step beyond a personal sense of inherent gross repulsiveness. Introjecting this repulsiveness—which she believes everyone except Bailey feels toward her—Maya generalizes on her role in Freeman's death and perceives herself as death's tool. "The only thing I could do," she reasons, "was to stop talking to people other than Bailey. Instinctively, or somehow, I knew that because I loved him so much I'd never hurt him, but if I talked to anyone else that person might die too. Just my breath, carrying my words out, might poison people and they'd curl up and die like the black fat slugs that only pretended" (73).

In this psychic state Maya conceives of her own body mythically as a Pandora's Box containing a degeneracy so virulent that, if left uncontrolled, will contaminate the universe. So profound is her hatred and rage, she recalls, that "I could feel the evilness flowing through my body and waiting, pent up, to rush off my tongue if I tried to open my mouth. I clamped my teeth shut, I'd hold it in. If it escaped, wouldn't it flood the world and all the innocent people" (72). As a vessel containing a death-inducing fluid, Maya must control the physical force within her with all the strength and will she can muster. Thus, her resolve not to speak and her consequent impassivity become outward manifestations of an inner struggle no less cosmic than Jacob's and the Angel's. This same struggle is the one that opens Angelou's autobiography.

Upon her return to Stamps, Maya projects her own deathlike inertness on the whole town. It is described as "exactly what I wanted, without will or consciousness. . . . Entering Stamps, I had the feeling that I was stepping over the border lines of the map and would fall, without fear, right off the end of the world. Nothing more could happen, for in Stamps nothing happened" (74).

An outcast in a community of outcasts, Maya avoids emotional ties with others. In fact, for six years, until Louise befriends her, Maya is without an intimate friend her own age. It is not surprising, then, that when Mrs. Bertha Flowers takes an active interest in her, Maya describes her as "the lady who threw me my first life line" (77). Nor is it surprising that Maya turns to the safety of books for the exciting relationships shunned in real life.

Yet, this pathological paralysis that inhibits Maya's ability to express her resentment and anger also opens the door to a gratification of her desire for a union with her mother. For Maya's passivity and obsession with death serve more than one unconscious need. While keeping her emotionally isolated from, and invulnerable to, others, they also gratify her regressive strivings for her mother.

Indeed, Maya's decision to lie at Freeman's trial was motivated not simply by mortal terror of her maternal clan and by fear of revealing her own complicity in the sexual episodes, but more important, by her desire for her mother's warmth and approving love.

> I couldn't say yes and tell them how he had loved me once for a few minutes and how he had held me close before he thought I had peed in my bed. My uncles would kill me and Grandmother Baxter would stop speaking, as she often did when she was angry. And all those people in the court would stone me as they had stoned the harlot in the Bible. And Mother, who thought I was such a good girl, would be so disappointed. . . .
>
> . . . I looked at his heavy face trying to look as if he would have liked me to say No. I said No.
>
> The lie lumped in my throat and I couldn't get air. . . . Our lawyer brought me off the stand and to my mother's arms. The fact that I had arrived at my desired destination by lies made it less appealing to me. (70–71)

When Maya's attempts at physical closeness with her mother—pathetically by way of Mr. Freeman's arms and her lie—prove unsuccessful, she reverts to the most primitive of all longings: to die. If death is "the condition in which identification with mother can be achieved," as Barchelon and Kovel postulate about *Huckleberry Finn*, then its "ultimate expression is passivity, of doing nothing." Thus, "in the unconscious, death can be represented as that dissolution of self necessary for reunion with the source of life, as a recapitulation of that self-less time in the womb."[10] Consequently, for a major portion of her autobiography, Maya Angelou evokes the notion of her willful dissolution—still another dimension in her book of the death-motif.

Thanatos, or the unconscious drive toward dissolution and death, exists in Angelou's narrative before the crucial episode of her rape and courtroom lie. Indeed, it first emerges when Maya is confronted with recognizing the existence of her parents. Deeply attached to the image of her dead mother, her indecision about joining the living one in St. Louis evokes the thought of suicide. "Should I go with father? Should I throw myself into the pond, and not being able to swim, join the body of L. C., the boy who had drowned last summer?" (46–47). Even her choice of method—death by water—calls up her yearning for a return to the source of all life, the mother.

Although her second residence in Stamps includes episodes wherein Maya considers her own death, these are generally handled more with humor than pathos. At any rate, the very abundance of references to her own extinction, regardless of Angelou's tone, is evidence of this theme's powerful hold over both the actor's and the author's unconscious. Three examples out of many will suffice. When cautioned by Mrs. Flowers to handle her books well, Maya can only imagine the most extreme punishment if she proves negligent: "Death would be too kind and brief" (82). Later, having survived to see the day of her graduation, Angelou relates, "Somewhere in my fatalism I had expected to die, accidentally, and never have the chance to walk up the stairs in the auditorium and gracefully receive my hard-earned diploma. Out of God's merciful bosom I had won reprieve" (147). Again, referring to the overwhelming sway books had over her and Bailey's imaginations, Angelou writes that "ever since we read *The Fall of the House of Usher,* we had made a pact that neither of us would allow the other to be buried without making 'absolutely, positively sure' (his favorite phrase) that the person was dead" (166).

Included in this part of her experience is Angelou's first conscious cognizance of her own mortality. So crucial an aspect of her identity is this awareness that Angelou devotes an entire chapter to it. Beneath the mock-Gothic melodrama of Mrs. Taylor's funeral and her posthumous nocturnal returns to visit her husband (neither of whom are mentioned again in the book) exists Maya's real and growing apprehension of her own mortal state: "I had never considered before that dying, death, dead, passed away, were words and phrases that might be even faintly connected with me" (135).

This deathward drift is arrested and altered when Maya moves to California. Just as Stamps reflects Maya's impassivity, so does San Francisco evoke her resiliency; while Stamps projects the worst side of Maya, so San Francisco affirms the best: "The city became for me the ideal of what I wanted to be as a grownup. Friendly but never gushing, cool but not frigid or distant, distinguished without the awful stiffness" (180). In San Francisco Maya's own identity happily merges with her environs. "In San Francisco, for the first time, I perceived myself as part of something," writes Angelou. "I identified . . . with the times and the city. . . . The undertone of fear that San Francisco would be bombed which was abetted by weekly air raid warnings, and civil defense drills in school, heightened my sense of belonging. Hadn't I, always, but ever and ever, thought that life was just one great risk for the living?" (179).

Death in its many manifestations is, indeed, pivotal to Maya Angelou's sense of self. But the life instinct, Eros, coexists with Thanatos in her autobiography, as it does in life. In fact, the tension between Maya's quest for a positive, life-affirming identity and her obsession with annihilation provides the unconscious dynamism affecting all aspects of her narrative and endowing it with power and conviction. Thus, the ultimate challenge to death is Maya's own active assertion of self and her willingness to face annihilation and overcome it. The remainder of Angelou's autobiography addresses itself to this end.

It is not until she visits Mexico with her father that Maya tenaciously struggles for her life. Leaving Maya to her own wits in a Mexican *cantina,* Bailey Johnson, Sr., takes off with his Mexican lover. When he finally returns, intoxicated beyond help, Maya must drive them both home. Although she has never driven, Maya defies and masters the bucking Hudson:

> The Hudson went crazy on the hill. It was rebelling and would have leaped over the side of the mountain, to all our destruction, in its attempt to unseat me had I relaxed control for a single second. The challenge was exhilarating. It was me, Marguerite, against the elemental opposition. As I twisted the steering wheel and forced the accelerator to the floor I was controlling Mexico, and might and aloneness and inexperienced youth and Bailey Johnson, Sr., and death and insecurity, and even gravity. (202–03)

But, as in the incident of Freeman's rape, the fatal pattern of reversal again appears. Maya's temporary safety is followed by Dolores's stabbing. When, in order to save face, Johnson hides Maya at a friend's home rather than bring her to a hospital, Maya is again confronted with the specter of her own death. She survives the night, however, sleeping "as if my death wish had come true" (212). But morning presents the inevitable questions: "What would I do? Did I have the nerve to commit suicide? If I jumped in the ocean wouldn't I come up all bloated like the man Bailey saw in Stamps?" (212). Although she has evoked her childish alternative of death by water and its unconscious wish for a return to mother, this time Maya resolves to make it on her own.

The decision not to retreat to her mother's home becomes the turning point in Maya Angelou's autobiography. "I could never succeed in shielding the gash in my side from her," she argues. "And if I failed to hide the wound we were certain to experience another scene of violence. I thought of poor Mr. Freeman, and the guilt which lined my heart, even after all those years, was a nagging passenger in my mind" (213). With this gesture, Maya not only triumphs over her regressive longing for death and mother but also, by sparing her father and Dolores, overcomes her sense of herself as death's tool.

Employing the same simile she had earlier used to describe her mother—"She was like a pretty kite that floated just above my head" (54)—Maya now describes herself as "a loose kite in a gentle wind floating with only my will for anchor" (214). Put more plainly, Maya rises in her own estimation, incorporates the best of her mother and becomes her own guardian. It is only then that Maya is ready to return to the human fold.

The outcast children of the dead-car junkyard where she seeks refuge eliminate Maya's "familiar insecurity," especially in relation to her mother. She learns "to drive . . . to curse and to dance" (215) with the best of them. But of signal importance is that these children disprove the racial prejudice—and its concurrent death fantasies—of her earlier experiences.

> After hunting down unbroken bottles and selling them with a white girl from Missouri, a Mexican girl from Los Angeles and a Black girl from Oklahoma, I was never again to sense myself so solidly outside the pale of the human race. The lack of criticism evidenced by our ad hoc community influenced me, and set a tone of tolerance for my life. (216)

That Angelou concludes her autobiography with the birth of her son is final evidence of the substantive power of death as metaphor of self in *I*

Know Why the Caged Bird Sings.[11] Her body, which she had earlier described as not only ugly and awkward but also contaminated with a death-inducing power, brings forth a living child. But the vestiges of her former self-image are not so easily excised. When her mother brings to Maya's bed her three-week-old baby, Maya is terror-stricken: "I was sure to roll over and crush out his life or break those fragile bones" (245). But later, when her mother wakens her, the apprehensive Maya discovers her son safe: "Under the tent of blanket, which was poled by my elbow and forearm, the baby slept touching my side" (246).

This final picture of Vivian Baxter as a confident and compassionate mother lovingly bent over her daughter's bed evokes the brown, nurturing figure of Maya's childhood fantasy. By asserting her faith in Maya's instinctive, preserving motherhood, Vivian Baxter not only qualifies the book's implicit image of her as cruel stepmother but also consummates Maya's growing sense of herself as an adult, life-giving woman.

When writing one's autobiography one's primary concern is the illumination of personal and historical identity while giving shape and meaning to the experiences out of which that identity has developed. Through the abyss of social and emotional death, Angelou emerges as a tenacious and vital individual. Indeed, in keeping with her death-and-rebirth fantasy, Maya Angelou is reborn: once, into a life-affirming identity recorded within the pages of her narrative, and again, when she re-creates that life as author of her autobiography. If one must enter a dark night of the soul in order to emerge radiant, then Maya Angelou's "terrible beauty" shines clear to the sky.

Notes

1. In the autobiography Angelou calls herself Maya or Marguerite Johnson, her given name. But, to avoid undue confusion, I have limited myself to the writer's signature. I do distinguish the child from the writer, however, and refer to the child as "Maya" and to the adult as "Angelou."

2. Maya Angelou, *I Know Why the Caged Bird Sings* (New York: Bantam Books, 1970), 1. Subsequent page references are to this edition.

3. Roy Pascal, *Design and Truth in Autobiography* (London: Routledge & Kegan Paul Ltd., 1960), 163.

4. Heinz Lichtenstein, "Identity and Sexuality: A Study of Their Interrelationship in Man," *Journal of the American Psychoanalytic Association* 9 (1961): 208.

5. Ibid., 253.

6. Ibid., 235.

7. Erik H. Erikson, *Childhood and Society* (New York: W. W. Norton & Company, 1963), 251.

8. All quotations referring to the anecdote are from pp. 1–3 of *I Know Why the Caged Bird Sings.*

9. William H. Grier and Price M. Cobbs, *Black Rage* (New York: Bantam Books, 1968), 51.

10. Jose Barchelon and Joel S. Kovel, *"Huckleberry Finn*: A Psychoanalytic Study," *Journal of the American Psychoanalytic Association* 22 (1966): 785.

11. Although the second volume of her autobiography, *Gather Together in My Name,* also contains the theme of death, it does not "open-up" the book the way it does her first. This supports (conveniently?) my contention that much of this theme is resolved in *I Know Why the Caged Bird Sings.* On the other hand, her book of verse, *Just Give Me a Cool Drink of Water 'fore I Diiie,* contains nineteen poems, out of a total thirty-eight, in which death is directly mentioned. Moreover, the theme of "mutability" echoes throughout her later works. One's "identity theme" is, indeed, irreversible.

Singing the Black Mother

Maya Angelou and Autobiographical Continuity

MARY JANE LUPTON

◆   ◆   ◆

> Now my problem I have is I love life, I love living
> life and I love the art of living, so I try to live my life
> as a poetic adventure, everything I do from the way
> I keep my house, cook, make my husband happy, or
> welcome my friends, raise my son; everything is
> part of a large canvas I am creating, I am living be-
> neath.
>
> (Chrisman, 46)

THIS ENERGETIC STATEMENT from a 1977 interview with
Maya Angelou merely hints at the variety of roles and experiences that
sweep through what is presently her five-volume autobiographical series: *I
Know Why the Caged Bird Sings* (1970), *Gather Together in My Name* (1974), *Singin' and
Swingin' and Gettin' Merry Like Christmas* (1976), *The Heart of a Woman* (1981), and *All
God's Children Need Traveling Shoes* (1986).[1] It is fitting that Angelou, so adept at
metaphor, should compare her "poetic adventure" to the act of painting:
"everything is part of a large canvas I am creating, I am living beneath."
Like an unfinished painting, the autobiographical series is an ongoing creation in a form that rejects the finality of a restricting frame. Its continuity
is achieved through characters who enter the picture, leave, and reappear
and through certain interlaced themes—self-acceptance, race, men, work,
separation, sexuality, motherhood. All the while Angelou lives "beneath,"
recording the minutest of details in a constantly shifting environment and
giving attention to the "mundane, though essential, ordinary moments of
life" (O'Neale, 34).

    I Know Why the Caged Bird Sings is the first and most highly praised volume in the series. It begins with the humiliations of childhood and ends with the birth of a child. At its publication, critics, not anticipating a series, readily appreciated the clearly developed narrative form. In 1973, for example, Sidonie Smith discussed the "sense of an ending" in *Caged Bird* as it relates to Angelou's acceptance of black womanhood: "With the birth of her child Maya is herself born into a mature engagement with the forces of life" (374). But with the introduction in 1974 of Angelou's second autobiographical volume, *Gather Together in My Name*, the tight structure appeared to crumble; childhood experiences were replaced by episodes that a number of critics consider disjointed or bizarre. Selwyn Cudjoe, for instance, noted the shift from the "intense solidity and moral center" in *Caged Bird* to the "conditions of *alienation* and *fragmentation*" in *Gather Together*, conditions that affect its organization and its quality, making it "conspicuously weak" (17, 20). Lynn Z. Bloom found the sequel "less satisfactory" because the narrator "abandons or jeopardizes the maturity, honesty, and intuitive good judgment toward which she had been moving in *Caged Bird*" (5). Crucial to Bloom's judgment is her concept of movement *toward*, which insinuates the achievement of an ending.

The narrator, as authentic recorder of the life, indeed changes during the second volume, as does the book's structure; the later volumes abandon the tighter form of *Caged Bird* for an episodic series of adventures whose so-called fragments are reflections of the kind of chaos found in actual living. In altering the narrative structure, Angelou shifts the emphasis from herself as an isolated consciousness to herself as a black woman participating in diverse experiences among a diverse class of peoples. As the world of experience widens, so does the canvas.

What distinguishes, then, Angelou's autobiographical method from more conventional autobiographical forms is her very denial of closure. The reader of autobiography expects a beginning, a middle, and an end— as occurs in *Caged Bird.* She or he also expects a central experience, as we indeed are given in the extraordinary rape sequence of *Caged Bird.* But Angelou, by continuing her narrative, denies the form and its history, creating from each ending a new beginning, relocating the center to some luminous place in a volume yet to be. Stretching the autobiographical canvas, she moves forward: from being a child; to being a mother; to leaving the child; to having the child, in the fifth volume, achieve his independence. Nor would I be so unwise as to call the fifth volume the end. For Maya Angelou, now a grandmother, has already published a moving, first-person account in *Woman's Day* of the four years of anguish surrounding the maternal kidnapping of her grandson Colin.

Throughout the more episodic volumes, the theme of motherhood remains a unifying element, with Momma Henderson being Angelou's link
with the black folk tradition—as George Kent, Elizabeth Schultz, and
other critics have mentioned. Since traditional solidity of development is
absent, one must sometimes search through three or four books to trace
Vivian Baxter's changing lovers, Maya Angelou's ambivalence toward
motherhood, or her son Guy's various reactions to his nontraditional upbringing. Nonetheless, the volumes are intricately related through a number of essential elements: the ambivalent autobiographical voice, the flexibility of structure to echo the life process, the intertextual commentary on
character and theme, and the use of certain recurring patterns to establish
both continuity and continuation. I have isolated the mother-child pattern as a way of approaching the complexity of Angelou's methods. One
could as well select other kinds of interconnected themes: the absent
and/or substitute father, the use of food as a psychosexual symbol, the dra-
matic/symbolic use of images of staring or gazing, and other motifs that establish continuity within and among the volumes.

Stephen Butterfield says of *Caged Bird:* "Continuity is achieved by the
contact of mother and child, the sense of life begetting life that happens
automatically in spite of all confusion—perhaps also because of it" (213).
The consistent yet changing connection for Maya Angelou through the
four subsequent narratives is that same contact of mother and child—with
herself and her son Guy; with herself and her own mother, Vivian Baxter;
with herself and her paternal grandmother; and, finally, with the child-
mother in herself.

Moreover, in extending the traditional one-volume form, Angelou has
metaphorically mothered another book. The "sense of life begetting life"
at the end of *Caged Bird* can no longer signal the conclusion of the narrative.
The autobiographical moment has been reopened and expanded; Guy's
birth can now be seen symbolically as the birth of another text. In a 1975 interview with Carol Benson, Angelou uses such a birthing metaphor in describing the writing of *Gather Together:* "If you have a child, it takes nine
months. It took me three-and-a-half years to write *Gather Together,* so I
couldn't just drop it" (19). This statement makes emphatic what in the autobiographies are much more elusive comparisons between creative work
and motherhood; after a three-and-a-half-year pregnancy she gives birth
to *Gather Together,* indicating that she must have planned the conception of
the second volume shortly after the 1970 delivery of *Caged Bird.*

Each of the five volumes explores, both literally and metaphorically,
the significance of motherhood. I will examine this theme from two

specific perspectives: first, Angelou's relationship to her mother and to mother substitutes, especially to Momma Henderson; second, Angelou's relationship to her son as she struggles to define her own role as mother/ artist. Throughout the volumes Angelou moves backward and forward, from connection to conflict. This dialectic of black mother-daughterhood, introduced in the childhood narrative, enlarges and contracts during the series, finding its fullest expression in *Singin' and Swingin' and Gettin' Merry Like Christmas*.

In flux, in defiance of chronological time, the mother-child configuration forms the basic pattern against which other relationships are measured and around which episodes and volumes begin or end. Motherhood also provides the series with a literary unity, as Angelou shifts positions— from mother to granddaughter to child—in a nonending text that, through its repetitions of maternal motifs, provides an ironic comment on her own sense of identity. For Angelou, despite her insistence on mother love, is trapped in the conflicts between working and mothering, independence and nurturing—conflicts that echo her ambivalence toward her mother, Vivian Baxter, and her apparent sanctification of Grandmother Henderson, the major adult figure in *Caged Bird*.

Annie Henderson is a solid, God-fearing, economically independent woman whose general store in Stamps, Arkansas, is the "lay center of activities in town" (*Caged Bird* 5), much as Annie is the moral center of the family. According to Mildred A. Hill-Lubin, the grandmother, both in Africa and in America, "has been a significant force in the stability and the continuity of the Black family and the community" (257). Hill-Lubin selects Annie Henderson as her primary example of the strong grandmother in African-American literature—the traditional preserver of the family, the source of folk wisdom, and the instiller of values within the black community. Throughout *Caged Bird* Maya has ambivalent feelings for this awesome woman, whose values of self-determination and personal dignity gradually chip away at Maya's dreadful sense of being "shit color" (17). As a self-made woman, Annie Henderson has the economic power to lend money to whites; as a practical black woman, however, she is convinced that whites cannot be directly confronted: "If she had been asked and had chosen to answer the question of whether she was cowardly or not, she would have said that she was a realist" (39). To survive in a racist society, Momma Henderson has had to develop a realistic strategy of submission that Maya finds unacceptable. Maya, in her need to re-image her grandmother, creates a metaphor that places Momma's power above any apparent submissiveness: Momma "did an excellent job of sagging from her waist down, but from the waist up she seemed to be pulling for the top of the oak tree across the road" (24).

There are numerous episodes, both in *Caged Bird* and *Gather Together,* that involve the conflict between Maya and her grandmother over how to deal with racism. When taunted by three "powhitetrash" girls, Momma quietly sings a hymn; Maya, enraged, would like to have a rifle (*Caged Bird* 23–27). Or, when humiliated by a white dentist who'd rather put his "hand in a dog's mouth than in a nigger's" (160), Annie is passive; Maya subsequently invents a fantasy in which Momma runs the dentist out of town. In the italicized dream text (161–62), Maya endows her grandmother with superhuman powers; Momma magically changes the dentist's nurse into a bag of chicken seed. In reality the grandmother has been defeated and humiliated, her only reward a mere ten dollars in interest for a loan she had made to the dentist (164). In Maya's fantasy Momma's *"eyes were blazing like live coals and her arms had doubled themselves in length";* in actuality she "looked tired" (162).

This richly textured passage is rendered from the perspective of an imaginative child who re-creates her grandmother—but in a language that ironically transforms Annie Henderson from a Southern black storekeeper into an eloquent heroine from a romantic novel: *"Her tongue had thinned and the words rolled off well enunciated."* Instead of the silent "nigra" (159) of the actual experience, Momma Henderson is now the articulate defender of her granddaughter against the stuttering dentist. Momma Henderson orders the *"contemptuous scoundrel"* to leave Stamps *"now and herewith."* The narrator eventually lets Momma speak normally, then comments: *"(She could afford to slip into the vernacular because she had such eloquent command of English.)"*

This fantasy is the narrator's way of dealing with her ambivalence toward Momma Henderson—a woman who throughout *Caged Bird* represents to Maya both strength and weakness, both generosity and punishment, both affection and the denial of affection. Here her defender is *"ten feet tall with eight-foot arms,"* quite capable, to recall the former tree image, of reaching the top of an oak from across the road. Momma's physical transformation in the dream text also recalls an earlier description: "I saw only her power and strength. She was taller than any woman in my personal world, and her hands were so large they could span my head from ear to ear" (38). In the dentist fantasy, Maya eliminates all of Momma Henderson's "negative" traits—submissiveness, severity, religiosity, sternness, down-home speech. It would seem that Maya is so shattered by her grandmother's reaction to Dentist Lincoln, so destroyed by her illusions of Annie Henderson's power in relationship to white people, that she compensates by reversing the true situation and having the salivating dentist be the target of Momma's wrath. Significantly, this transformation occurs immediately before Momma Henderson tells Maya and Bailey that they are going to California. Its position in the text gives it the impression of finality. Any negative attitudes become submerged, only to surface later, in *Gather Together*, as aspects of Angelou's own ambiguity toward race, power, and identity.

In *Caged Bird* Momma Henderson had hit Maya with a switch for unknowingly taking the Lord's name in vain, "like whitefolks do" (87). Similarly, in *Gather Together* Annie slaps her granddaughter after Maya, on a visit to Stamps, verbally assaults two white saleswomen. In a clash with Momma Henderson that is both painful and final, Maya argues for "the principle of the thing," and Momma slaps her.[2] Surely, Momma's slap is well intended; she wishes to protect Maya from "lunatic cracker boys" and men in white sheets, from all of the insanity of racial prejudice (78–79). The "new" Maya, who has been to the city and found a sense of independence, is caught in the clash between her recently acquired "principles" and Momma's fixed ideology. Thus the slap—but also the intention behind it—will remain in Maya's memory long after the mature Angelou has been separated from Annie Henderson's supervision. Momma makes Maya and the baby leave Stamps, again as a precaution: "Momma's intent to protect me had caused her to hit me in the face, a thing she had never done, and to send me away to where she thought I'd be safe" (79). Maya departs on the train, never to see her grandmother again.

In the third volume Angelou, her marriage falling apart, is recuperating from a difficult appendectomy. When she tells her husband Tosh that she wants to go to Stamps until she is well, he breaks the news that Annie Henderson died the day after Angelou's operation. In recording her reaction to her grandmother's death, Angelou's style shifts from its generally more conversational tone and becomes intense, religious, emotional:

> Ah, Momma. I had never looked at death before, peered into its yawning chasm for the face of the beloved. For days my mind staggered out of balance. I reeled on a precipice of knowledge that even if I were rich enough to travel all over the world, I would never find Momma. If I were as good as God's angels and as pure as the Mother of Christ, I could never have Momma's rough slow hands pat my cheek or braid my hair.
>
> Death to the young is more than that undiscovered country; despite its inevitability, it is a place having reality only in song or in other people's grief. (*Singin' and Swingin'*, 41)

This moving farewell, so atypical of Angelou's more worldly autobiographical style, emerges directly from a suppressed religious experience that Angelou narrates earlier in the same text—a "secret crawl through neighborhood churches" (28). These visits, done without her white husband's knowledge, culminate in Angelou's being saved at the Evening Star Baptist Church. During her purification, Angelou cries for her family: "For my fatherless son, who was growing up with a man who would never, could never, understand his need for manhood; for my mother, whom I admired but didn't understand; for my brother, whose disappointment with life was drawing him relentlessly into the clutches of death; and, finally, I cried for myself, long and loudly" (33). Annie Henderson is strangely absent from this list of family for whom Angelou cries during the short-lived conversion. But only a few pages later, Angelou remembers her grandmother's profound importance, in the elegiac passage on Momma's death.

In this passage Angelou creates a funeral song that relies on the black gospel tradition, on the language of Bible stories, and on certain formative literary texts.[3] Words like *chasm, precipice, angels,* and *beloved* have Sunday School overtones, a kind of vocabulary Angelou more typically employs for humorous effects, as in the well-known portrait of Sister Monroe (*Caged Bird,* 32–37).[4] The gospel motif, so dominant in the passage, seems directly related to Angelou's rediscovery of the black spiritual: "The spirituals and gospel songs were sweeter than sugar. I wanted to keep my mouth full of them and the sounds of my people singing fell like sweet oil in my ears" (*Singing' and Swingin',* 28). During her conversion experience Angelou lies on the floor while four women march round her singing, "Soon one morning when death comes walking in my room" (33); in another spiritual the singers prepare for the "walk to Jerusalem" (31). These and similar hymns about death had been significant elements of the "folk religious tradition" of Momma Henderson (Kent, 76). Now, for a brief time, they become part of the mature Angelou's experience. That their revival is almost immediately followed by the death of Momma Henderson accounts, to a large extent, for Angelou's intensely religious narrative.

Angelou's singing of the black grandmother in this passage contains other refrains from the past, most notably her desire to have "Momma's rough slow hands pat my cheek." These are the same hands that slapped Maya for having talked back to the white saleswomen—an event that was physically to separate grandmother and granddaughter (*Gather Together,* 86–88). That final slap, softened here, becomes a loving pat on the cheek akin to a moment in *Caged Bird* in which Maya describes her grandmother's love as a touch of the hand: "Just the gentle pressure of her rough hand conveyed her own concern and assurance to me" (96). Angelou's tone throughout the elegy is an attempt, through religion, to reconcile her ambivalence toward Momma Henderson by sharing her traditions. Angelou wishes to be "as good as God's angels" and as "pure as the Mother of Christ," metaphors that seem to represent Angelou's effort to close off the chasm between herself and Momma Henderson through the use of a common language, the language of the churchgoing grandmother.

As Momma Henderson, the revered grandmother, recedes from the narrative, Angelou's natural mother gains prominence. By the third volume Maya Angelou and Vivian Baxter have established a closeness that somewhat compensates for Maya's having been sent off to Stamps as a child, a situation so painful that Maya had imagined her mother dead:

> I could cry anytime I wanted by picturing my mother (I didn't quite know what she looked like) lying in her coffin. . . . The face was brown, like a big O, and since I couldn't fill in the features I printed M O T H E R across the O, and tears would fall down my cheeks like warm milk. (*Caged Bird,* 42–43)

Like Maya's fantasy of her grandmother and Dentist Lincoln, the above passage is an imaginative revision of reality, Maya's way to control the frustrations produced by Vivian's rejection. The images of the dream text invoke romance fiction and Amazonian strength. Here the images concern, first, the artist who fills in the empty canvas (the O) with print; second, the motherlike child who cries tears of "warm milk" in sympathy for her imagined dead mother. These interlaced metaphors of writing and nurturance appear frequently in the continuing text, as Angelou explores her relationships with mothers and children.

When Maya is eight years old, she and Bailey visit their mother in St. Louis, where Maya discovers her exquisite beauty: "To describe my mother would be to write about a hurricane in its perfect power. Or the climbing, falling colors of a rainbow. . . . She was too beautiful to have children" (*Caged Bird,* 49–50). Ironically, this mother "too beautiful to have children" is to a large degree responsible for her own child's brutal rape. Vivian's beauty attracts a lover, Mr. Freeman, who is constantly in the house waiting for a woman who is not there, and he "uses Angelou as an extension of her mother" to satisfy his sexual urges (Demetrakopoulos, 198). It could also be suggested that Vivian uses Maya, somehow knowing that in her own absence Maya will keep her lover amused. When Maya becomes ill, Vivian responds in a motherly manner: making broth, cooking Cream of Wheat, taking Maya's temperature, calling a doctor. After she discovers the rape, Vivian sends Maya to a hospital, bringing her flowers and candy (*Caged Bird,* 69).

It is Grandmother Baxter, however, who sees to it that the rapist is punished; after the trial a policeman comes to the house and informs an unsurprised Mrs. Baxter that Freeman has been kicked to death. Mrs. Baxter is a political figure in St. Louis, a precinct captain and gambler whose light skin and "six mean children" bring her both power and respect (51). Like Momma Henderson, Grandmother Baxter is a source of strength for Maya. Both grandmothers are "strong, independent[,] skillful women who are able to manage their families and to insure their survival in a segregated and hostile society" (Hill-Lubin, 260).

Despite their positive influence, however, Maya has ambivalent feelings toward her powerful grandmothers. Maya feels guilty for having lied at the trial, a guilt compounded when she learns of Grandmother Baxter's part in Freeman's murder. To stop the "poison" in her breath, Maya retreats into a "perfect personal silence," which neither of the Baxter women can penetrate and which Maya breaks only for Bailey (73). The disastrous St. Louis sequence stops abruptly, without transition: "We were on the train going back to Stamps . . ." (74). Thus, the end of the visit to Grandmother Baxter parallels chapter one of *Caged Bird;* a train moves from an urban center to rural Arkansas and to the protection of Annie Henderson.

Back at her grandmother's general store, Maya meets Mrs. Bertha Flowers, "the aristocrat of Black Stamps" (77). This unambivalently positive mother figure helps Maya to recover her oral language through the written text—reading *A Tale of Two Cities.* In a series of sharp contrasts, the narrator conveys Maya's divided feelings between the sophisticated mother figure, Mrs. Flowers, and her more provincial grandmother. Mrs. Flowers wears gloves, whereas Mrs. Henderson has rough hands. Mrs. Flowers admires white male writers, whereas Annie Henderson will not tolerate them. And in a set of contrasts that occurs almost simultaneously in the text, the literary Mrs. Flowers rewards Maya's language with sweets, whereas the religious grandmother punishes Maya's spoken words ("by the way") without making any effort to explain her anger. In an earlier passage, however, the narrator merges these basic oppositions into a dynamic interaction between two black women: "I heard the soft-voiced Mrs. Flowers and the textured voice of my grandmother merging and melting. They were interrupted from time to time by giggles that must have come from Mrs. Flowers (Momma never giggled in her life). Then she was gone" (79). These contrasts appear following Maya's failed relationship with Vivian Baxter. They are indications of the split mother—

the absent natural mother, the gentle Mrs. Flowers, the forceful Annie Henderson— whose divisions Angelou must articulate if she is to find her own autobiographical voice.

Although most critics have seen a wholeness in Maya's personality at the conclusion of *Caged Bird,* a few have observed this division of self, which Demetrakopoulos relates to Maya's conflicts about the mother: she "splits the feminine archetype of her mother's cold Venus and her grandmother's primal warm sheltering Demeter aspects" (198). The Jungian metaphors may jar in this African-American context, but I agree with Demetrakopoulos that at the end of *Caged Bird* the narrator is split. She is a mother who is herself a child; a daughter torn by her notions of mother love; an uncertain black teenager hardly capable of the heavy burden of closure placed on her by Sidonie Smith, Stephen Butterfield, Selwyn Cudjoe, and other critics.

Nor is this split mended when Angelou gives birth to *Gather Together.* Here she introduces herself by way of contradictions: "I was seventeen, very old, embarrassingly young, with a son of two months, and I still lived with my mother and stepfather" (3). Vivian Baxter intermittently takes care of Guy while his young mother works as a cook or shopkeeper. When Momma Henderson forces Maya and her son to leave Stamps, they go immediately to the security of Vivian's fourteen-room house in San Francisco. One gets a strong sense throughout *Gather Together* of Maya's dependence on her mother. Angelou admires her mother for her self-reliance, her encouragement, and her casual approach to sexuality. She also continues to be captivated by Vivian's beauty, by her "snappy-fingered, head-tossing elegance" (*Singin' and Swingin',* 70). On the other hand, she recognizes Vivian Baxter's flaws: "Her own mind was misted by the knowledge of a failing marriage, and the slipping away of the huge sums of money which she had enjoyed and thought her due" (*Gather Together,* 24).

As for her son, Angelou reveals similar contradictory feelings. After quitting a job to be with Guy, Angelou writes: "A baby's love for his mother is probably the sweetest emotion we can savor" (*Gather Together,* 90). In a more depressed mood, however, she comments that her child's disposition had "lost its magic to make me happy" (174). What Angelou does in these instances is to articulate her feelings as they convey the reality of her experiences, even though some of these negative emotions might not represent her best side.

The most dramatic mother-child episode in *Gather Together* occurs while Angelou is working as a prostitute. She leaves Guy with her sitter, Big Mary. Returning for Guy after several days, she learns that her son has been kidnapped. Angelou finally recovers her child, unharmed; at that moment she realizes that they are both separate individuals and that Guy is not merely a "beautiful appendage of myself" (163), Angelou's awareness of the inevitable separation of mother and child, expressed here for the first time, is a theme that she will continue to explore through the remaining autobiographical volumes.

Gather Together closes with Angelou's and Guy's returning to the protection of Vivian Baxter, following Angelou's glimpse at the horrors of heroin addiction: "I had no idea what I was going to make of my life, but I had given a promise and found my innocence. I swore I'd never lose it again" (181). In its tableau of mother, child, and grandmother, this concluding paragraph directly parallels the ending of *Caged Bird*.

In the next volume, *Singin' and Swingin'*, the closeness between mother and daughter continues. As she matures, Angelou becomes more in control of her feelings and more objective in her assessment of Vivian Baxter's personality. Additionally, the separation of egos that Angelou perceived after locating her kidnapped son would extend to the mother-daughter and grandmother-granddaughter relationships as well. But *Singin' and Swingin' and Gettin' Merry Like Christmas* is, despite its joyful title, a mesh of conflicts—many of them existing within the autobiographical self; many of them involving separations that, although consciously chosen, become unbearable. A number of ambiguities appear throughout the book, especially as they concern the mother-child pattern that is to dominate this and the subsequent texts.

The underlying drama in *Singin' and Swingin'* is played out between Angelou, the single parent of a young son, and Angelou, the actress who chooses to leave that son with Vivian Baxter in order to tour Europe with the company of *Porgy and Bess*. Angelou is keenly aware that putting Guy in the care of his grandmother is an echo of her own child-mother experience:

> The past revisited. My mother had left me with my grandmother for years and I knew the pain of parting. My mother, like me, had had her motivations, her needs. I did not relish visiting the same anguish on my son, and she, years later, told me how painful our separation was to her. But I had to work and I had to be good. I would make it up to my son and one day would take him to all the places I was going to see. (129)

Angelou's feelings are compounded by the fact that, as a young, black, single mother, she alone is finally responsible for giving her child a sense of stability.[5] In identifying the conflict between working and mothering, Angelou offers a universalized representation of the turmoil that may arise when a woman attempts to fulfill both roles.

Angelou suffers considerably on the European tour. In some instances her longings for Guy make her sleep fitfully (147) or make her distracted—as when she sees some young Italian boys with "pale-gold complexions" who remind her of her son (148). When she is paged at a Paris train station, Angelou fears that something dreadful has happened to Guy, and she blames herself: "I knew I shouldn't have left my son. There was a telegram waiting for me to say he had been hurt somehow. Or had run away from home. Or had caught an awful disease" (151–52). On other occasions she speaks quite directly of her guilt: "I sent my dollars home to pay for Clyde's [Guy's] keep and to assuage my guilt at being away from him" (153).[6]

Of the many examples in *Singin' and Swingin'* that address this conflict, I have selected one particular passage to illustrate the ways in which Angelou articulates her ambivalence about mothering. While she is in Paris, Angelou earns extra money by singing in a nightclub and decides to send the money home rather than spend it on a room with a private bath: "Mom could buy something wonderful for Clyde every other week and tell him I'd sent it. Then perhaps he would forgive my absence" (157). The narrator shows no qualms about lying to her son; Vivian could "tell him I'd sent it." Additionally, she makes no connection between her efforts to buy forgiveness and the anger she felt as a child when her absent mother, the same "Mom" of the above passage, sent Maya a tea set and a doll with yellow hair for Christmas: "Bailey and I tore the stuffing out of the doll the day after Christmas, but he warned me that I had to keep the tea set in good condition because any day or night she might come riding up" (*Caged Bird*, 43). Liliane K. Arensberg interprets the tea cups as "symbols of a white world beyond Maya's reach of everyday experience," whereas the torn doll "serves as an effigy of her mother by virtue of being female and a gift" (281). Although I agree with Arensberg's interpretation, I tend to read the gifts as metaphors for Maya's divided self. The preserved tea set, the torn doll—what better signifiers could there be for the split feelings of the abandoned child, who destroys one gift to show anger but saves the other in anticipation of the mother's return? I would also suggest that the seemingly inappropriate title *Singin' and Swingin' and Gettin' Merry Like Christmas* may be intended to signal the reader back to the very unmerry Christmas of *Caged Bird.*

In the Paris sequence the narrator seems to have suppressed, in her role as *mother*, some of the anguish she had experienced during childhood—

although in the passage previously cited (*Singin' and Swingin'*, 129), she recognizes the similarities between her own "pains of parting" and her son's. Angelou refers to this separation from her son so frequently in the text that he becomes a substantial part of the narrative, the source of Angelou's guilt but also the major factor in the development of dramatic tension. Angelou, in this most complex of the autobiographies, is richly and honestly rendering the split in her own psyche between being a "good" mother (being at home) and being a "bad" mother (selfishly staying in Europe). The narrator pretends to herself that her son wants a gift, thus prolonging the admission that he really wants his mother—as Maya had wanted hers.

To arrive at this interpretation the reader must move back and forth among the texts, perceiving parallels in order to decipher the narrator's motivations. The frequent references in *Singin' and Swingin'* to separation and to guilt give one considerable access to the narrator's complex personality; at the same time, these references demand to be read against and with the entire series—intertextuality in its strictest sense.

Angelou returns from Europe to find her son suffering from a skin disease that is an overt expression of his loneliness. In a promise that recalls the last lines of *Gather Together* (never again to lose her innocence), Angelou vows to Guy: "I swear to you, I'll never leave you again. If I go, you'll go with me or I won't go" (*Singin' and Swingin'*, 232). She takes Guy with her to Hawaii, where she has a singing engagement. *Singin' and Swingin'* closes in a sentence that highlights, through its three nouns, the underlying tensions of the book: "Although I was not a great *singer* I was his *mother*, and he was my wonderful, dependently independent *son*" (242, emphasis added). Dialectical in phrasing, this statement not only functions to close the first three books but also opens itself to the mother-son patterns of the future volumes: fluctuations between dependence and independence.

In *The Heart of a Woman* the tension between mothering and working continues, but to a lesser extent. Guy is now living with his mother and not with Vivian Baxter. But Angelou, despite her earlier vow, does occasionally leave her son. During a night club engagement in Chicago, Angelou trusts Guy to the care of her friend John Killens. One night Killens phones from Brooklyn and informs her that "there's been some trouble" (75). In a moment of panic that recalls her fears at the Paris train station (*Gather Together*, 151–52), Angelou again imagines that Guy has been injured, stolen, "struck by an errant bus, hit by a car out of control" (75).[7]

Angelou confronts these fears in the Brooklyn adventure, the most dramatic episode of *The Heart of a Woman*. Unlike the internal conflicts of

Gather Together, this one operates outside of the narrator, showing Maya Angelou as a strong, aggressive black mother rather than a mother torn by
self-doubt. While Angelou was in Chicago, Guy had gotten in trouble with
a Brooklyn street gang. In order to protect her son, she confronts Jerry, the
gang leader, and threatens to shoot his entire family if Guy is harmed.
Jerry's response is an ironic comment on the motherhood theme of the
autobiographies: "O.K., I understand. But for a mother, I must say you're a
mean motherfucker" (84). Powerful, protective of her son, Angelou has
become in this episode a reincarnation of Momma Henderson.

Unfortunately, no mother or grandmother or guardian angel, no matter how strong, can keep children forever from danger. Near the end of *The
Heart of a Woman,* Guy is seriously injured in a car accident. In a condensed,
tormented autobiographical passage, Angelou gazes at the face of her unconscious son and summarizes their life together:

> He was born to me when I was seventeen. I had taken him away from my
> mother's house when he was two years old, and except for a year I spent in
> Europe without him, and a month when he was stolen by a deranged
> woman, we had spent our lives together. My grown life lay stretched before
> me, stiff as a pine board, in a strange country, blood caked on his face and
> clotted on his clothes. (263)[8]

Guy gradually recovers, moving, during the process of physical healing,
toward a position of greater independence from his mother.

But Angelou, too, moves towards a separateness, much as she had predicted in *Gather Together* (163). In *The Heart of a Woman* the texture of Angelou's
life changes significantly. She travels a lot, seeing far less of Vivian—
although she does write to her mother from Ghana asking for financial help
after Guy's accident (268). She strengthens her public identity, becoming a
coordinator in the civil rights movement and a professionally recognized
dancer and actress. She also, for the first time in the autobiographies, begins
her account of self as writer. Angelou attends a writer's workshop; publishes
a short story; becomes friends with John Killens, Rosa Guy, Paule Marshall,
and other black novelists. Most important, writing forces her into a conscious maturity: "If I wanted to write, I had to be willing to develop a kind of
concentration found mostly in people awaiting execution. I had to learn
technique and surrender my ignorance" (41). By extension, the rich ambivalence of *Singin 'and Swingin'* could only have been achieved by a writer who had
abandoned "ignorance" for a conscious self-exploration.

Paradoxically, the independent writer/mother establishes this "kind of
concentration" in maternal solitude. *Singin' and Swingin'* had ended with

mother and son reunited, both dependent and independent. *The Heart of a Woman* ends in separation. Guy, now a student at the University of Ghana, is moving to a dormitory. In the last two paragraphs we find Angelou alone:

> I closed the door and held my breath. Waiting for the wave of emotion to surge over me, knock me down, take my breath away. Nothing happened. I didn't feel bereft or desolate. I didn't feel lonely or abandoned. I sat down, still waiting. The first thought that came to me, perfectly formed and promising, was "At last, I'll be able to eat the whole breast of a roast chicken by myself." (272)

Angelou's reaction to having "closed the door" on her son is, like so many of her feelings in this complicated relationship, ambivalent. The language of the passage is initially charged with negativity: "Nothing happened. I didn't feel. . . . I didn't feel. . . ." The son she had loved through all of "our lives together" (263) is gone. Angelou sits waiting for something dreadful to happen to herself—as she had earlier imagined Guy's being stolen or being hit by a bus. But the narrator counters this negative attitude with a note of irony in which she reverses the biological assumption of the mother as she-who-nourishes: She can now have the "whole breast" to herself.

The family chicken dinner is a recurring motif in the autobiographical series. Recall the marvelous scene from *Caged Bird* in which Maya and Bailey watch Reverend Howard Thomas gobble down Momma Henderson's chicken dinner: "He ate the biggest, brownest and best parts of the chicken at every Sunday meal" (28). Now there is no competition. Angelou has the best part, the breast, to herself. On the negative side, Angelou is left, at the end of the fourth volume, in isolation; the last word of *The Heart of a Woman* is "myself." But the negativity is outweighed by the more "promising" aspects of being alone, the word *promising* an echo of the resolutions of *Gather Together* and *Singin' and Swingin'*, which end in vows of innocence and of commitment. The "perfectly formed" thought at the end of *The Heart of a Woman* is Angelou's realization of a new "myself," of a woman no longer primarily defined as granddaughter or daughter or mother—a woman free to choose herself.

All God's Children Need Traveling Shoes opens by going back in time to Angelou the mother, who anxiously waits at the hospital following Guy's car accident. In an image that parodies the well-fed mother of *The Heart of a Woman*, Angelou compares her anxiety over Guy to being eaten up:

July and August of 1962 stretched out like fat men yawning after a sumptuous dinner. They had every right to gloat, for they had eaten me up. Gobbled me down. Consumed my spirit, not in a wild rush, but slowly, with the obscene patience of certain victors. I became a shadow walking in the white hot streets; and a dark spectre in the hospital. (4)

The months of helplessly waiting for Guy to heal are like fat, stuffed men, a description that evokes memories of Reverend Thomas, who ate Momma Henderson's chicken, and of Mr. Freeman, who ate in Vivian Baxter's kitchen and raped her daughter. Guy's accident has an effect similar to the rape; Angelou retreats into silence. She is a "shadow," a "dark spectre," a black mother silenced by the fear of her son's possible death.

Guy does recover. Their relationship, which like the autobiographical form itself is constantly in flux, moves once again from dependence to independence, climaxing in a scene in which Angelou learns that her son is having an affair with an American woman a year older than herself. Angelou at first threatens to strike him, but Guy merely pats her head and says: "Yes, little mother. I'm sure you will" (149). Shortly afterward Angelou travels to Germany to perform in Genet's *The Blacks*. Guy meets her return flight and takes her home to a dinner of fried chicken he has cooked for her. Then, asserting his independence, he announces that he has "plans for dinner" (186).

Reading between the texts, we see Angelou alone again before a plate of chicken, as she was at the conclusion of *The Heart of a Woman*. In the *Traveling Shoes* episode, however, the conflicting feelings of love and resentment are more directly stated:

> He's gone. My lovely little boy is gone and will never return. That big confident strange man has done away with my little boy, and he has the gall to say he loves me. How can he love me? He doesn't know me, and I sure as hell don't know him. (186)

In this passage Angelou authentically faces and records the confusions of seeing one's child achieve selfhood, universalizing the pain a mother experiences when her "boy" is transformed into a "big confident strange man" who refuses to be his mother's "beautiful appendage" (*Gather Together*, 162).

Yet through much of the fifth volume, Angelou continues to separate herself from Guy and to form new relationships. She shares experiences with other women, including her two roommates; she befriends an African boy named Koko; she enjoys her contacts with the colony of black American writers and artists living in Ghana; and she continues her sexual involvements with men. The love affair that seems most vital in *Traveling Shoes*, however, is with Africa herself. In her travels through West Africa Angelou discovers certain connections between her own traditions and those of her African ancestors. She takes great satisfaction in her heritage when she is mistaken for a Bambara woman. Among African women she discovers strong mother figures, most notably Patience Aduah, whose custom of giving away food by the campfire evokes memories of Momma Henderson's having shared her table with black American travelers denied rooms in hotels or seats in restaurants during the era of segregation in much of America (*Traveling Shoes*, 102). Through her identification with Africa, Angelou reaffirms the meaning of motherhood.[9]

Although captivated by the oral traditions of Mother Africa, Angelou chooses to leave, at the conclusion of *Traveling Shoes*, in order to return to the rhythms of Southern black churches, the rhythms of her grandmother. In so doing, however, she must also leave her son. The final scene in the book is at the Accra airport. Angelou is saying farewell to her friends and, most specifically, to Guy, who "stood, looking like a young lord of summer, straight, sure among his Ghanaian companions" (208). Through this suggestion of Guy as an African prince, Angelou roots him in the culture of West Africa.

If we look at the closure of *Traveling Shoes* on a literal level, then Angelou's son is a college student, staying on to complete his degree. But if we accept a grander interpretation, Guy has become, through his interaction with the Ghanaians, a "young lord" of Africa, given back to the Mother Continent freely, not lost, like so many other children, in Midpassage or in slavery. Angelou lovingly accepts the separation, knowing that "someone like me and certainly related to me" will be forming new bonds between himself and Mother Africa (209). Guy is making an essentially free choice that centuries of black creativity in America have helped make possible: "Through the centuries of despair and dislocation we had been creative, because we faced down death by daring to hope" (208).

As in the four earlier autobiographies, this one closes with the mother-son configuration. But in the final, puzzling line of *Traveling Shoes* Angelou swings the focus away from Guy and towards the edge of the canvas: "I could nearly hear the old ones chuckling" (209). In this spiritual call to her ancestors Angelou imaginatively connects herself to the Ketans and the Ghanaians, to the people placed in chains, to all of God's children who had "never completely left Africa" (209). Ironically, the narrator herself has not completely left Africa either. The rhythmic prose that concludes the fifth volume is an anticipated departure to a new world, with the narrator still at the airport. As in the other volumes, the closure is thus another opening into the next narrative journey.

Notes

1. I use the name *Maya* in discussing the protagonist either as child or as the young woman of *Gather Together*. When I refer to the mature woman or to the narrator, I use *Angelou* or *Maya Angelou*.

2. In Fielder Cook's 1978 Learning Corporation of America teleplay of *Caged Bird*, the slap occurs following Annie Henderson's confrontation with the "powhitetrash" girls. Maya, played by Constance Good, says: "I would tell them to go to Hell. I would spit on their faces." Momma, played by Esther Rolle, soundly slaps Maya. The corrective slap is of course not unique in black drama; the same actress, Esther Rolle, slaps her daughter for blaspheming in the 1988 production of Lorraine Hansberry's *A Raisin in the Sun* directed by Harold Scott at the Morris A. Mechanic Theatre in Baltimore.

3. I wish to thank Nellie McKay and Julia Lupton, respectively, for pointing out to me the echoes of James Weldon Johnson and William Shakespeare in this passage. In Johnson's "Go Down Death—A Funeral Sermon," Jesus "smoothed the furrows" from Sister Caroline's face while angels sing to her. Angelou incorporates these images into her own funeral sermon. Angelou's comparison of death to "that undiscovered country" is a direct allusion to *Hamlet* (3.1.79–80): "The undiscover'd country from whose bourn / No traveller returns." These references, then, are further articulations of the conflicts in language and culture that Angelou introduces in *Caged Bird* (11); to please their grandmother, Maya and Bailey would recite from Johnson's "The Creation" and not from Shakespeare's *The Merchant of Venice*.

4. See Stephen Butterfield, who discusses Angelou's sense of humor in the church scenes of *Caged Bird* and compares it to humorous techniques used by Langston Hughes and James Weldon Johnson (209).

5. According to Carol E. Neubauer, Angelou "identifies her own situation and the threat of displacement as a common condition among black families in America and acknowledges the special responsibilities of the black mother" (124).

6. *Guy* is the name Angelou's son chooses for himself (*Singin' and Swingin'*, 237–38) instead of *Clyde*, the name he was given at birth.

7. In her study of style and displacement in *The Heart of a Woman*, Carol E. Neubauer discusses the Killens phone call and other episodes as aspects of a "pattern of fantasy" through which Angelou reveals "the vulnerability she feels as a mother trying to protect her child from any form of danger" (128).

8. The "strange country" of this passage recalls the "undiscovered country" of the elegy to Annie Henderson.

9. Like David Diop, Léopold Senghor, and other contemporary African writers included in *The African Assertion,* Angelou adopts the image of Africa as mother, expressing this image through the African oral tradition rather than through her own written reflections. Thus Angelou has Ghanaian chief Nana Nketsia extol Mother Africa in "a rhythm reminiscent of preachers in Southern Black churches" (*Traveling Shoes,* 112).

Works Cited

Angelou, Maya. *All God's Children Need Traveling Shoes* (New York: Random House, [1986] 1987).

————. *Gather Together in My Name* (New York: Bantam, [1974] 1975).

————. *The Heart of a Woman* (New York: Bantam, [1981] 1982).

————. *I Know Why the Caged Bird Sings* (New York: Bantam, [1970] 1971).

————. "My Grandson, Home at Last." *Woman's Day.* Aug. 1986, 46–55.

————. *Singin' and Swingin' and Gettin' Merry Like Christmas* (New York: Bantam, [1976] 1977).

Arensberg, Liliane K. "Death as Metaphor of Self in *I Know Why the Caged Bird Sings.*" *College Language Association Journal* 20 (1976): 273–96.

Benson, Carol. "Out of the Cage and Still Singing." *Writer's Digest.* Jan. 1975, 18–20.

Bloom, Lynn Z. "Maya Angelou." *Dictionary of Literary Biography.* Vol. 38. (Detroit: Gale, 1985), 3–12.

Butterfield, Stephen. *Black Autobiography in America* (Amherst: Univ. of Massachusetts Press, 1974).

Chrisman, Robert. "*The Black Scholar* Interviews Maya Angelou." *Black Scholar* (Jan.–Feb. 1977): 44–52.

Cudjoe, Selwyn. "Maya Angelou and the Autobiographical Statement." *Black Women Writers (1950–1980): A Critical Evaluation.* Ed. Mari Evans (Garden City: Doubleday, 1984), 6–24.

Demetrakopoulos, Stephanie A. "The Metaphysics of Matrilinearism in Women's Autobiography: Studies of Mead's *Blackberry Winter,* Hellman's *Pentimento,* Angelou's *I Know Why the Caged Bird Sings,* and Kingston's *The Woman Warrior.*" *Women's Autobiography: Essays in Criticism.* Ed. Estelle Jelinek (Bloomington: Indiana Univ. Press, 1980), 180–205.

Hill-Lubin, Mildred A. "The Grandmother in African and African-American Literature: A Survivor of the Extended Family," in *Ngambika: Studies of Women in African Literature.* Ed. Carole B. Davies and Anne A. Graves (Trenton: Africa World, 1986), 257–70.

Kent, George E. "*I Know Why the Caged Bird Sings* and Black Autobiographical Tradition." *Kansas Quarterly* 7, no.3 (1975): 72–78.

Neubauer, Carol E. "Displacement and Autobiographical Style in Maya Angelou's *The Heart of a Woman." Black American Literature Forum* 17 (1983): 123–29.

O'Neale, Sondra. "Reconstruction of the Composite Self: New Images of Black Women in Maya Angelou's Continuing Autobiography," in *Black Women Writers (1950–1980): A Critical Evaluation.* Ed. Mari Evans (Garden City: Doubleday, 1984), 25–36.

Schultz, Elizabeth. "To Be Black and Blue: The Blues Genre in Black American Autobiography." *Kansas Quarterly* 7, no. 3 (1975): 81–96.

Shelton, Austin J., ed. *The African Assertion: A Critical Anthology of African Literature* (Indianapolis: Odyssey, 1968).

Smith, Sidonie. "The Song of a Caged Bird: Maya Angelou's Quest after Self-Acceptance." *Southern Humanities Review* 7 (1973): 365–75.

Maya Angelou

An Interview

CLAUDIA TATE

◆ ◆ ◆

M AYA ANGELOU: Image making is very important for every
human being. It is especially important for black American women
in that we are, by being black, a minority in the United States, and by being
female, the less powerful of the genders. So, we have two areas we must
address. If we look out of our eyes at the immediate world around us, we
see whites and males in dominant roles. We need to see our mothers,
aunts, our sisters, and grandmothers. We need to see Frances Harper, So-
journer Truth, Fannie Lou Hammer, women of our heritage. We need to
have these women preserved. We need them all: . . . Constance Motley,
Etta Motten. . . . All of these women are important as role models. Depending on our profession, some may be even more important. Zora Neale
Hurston means a great deal to me as a writer. So does Josephine Baker, but
not in the same way because her profession is not directly related to mine.
Yet I would imagine for someone like Diahann Carroll or Diana Ross, Miss
Baker must mean a great deal. I would imagine that Bessie Smith and
Mammie Smith, though they are important to me, would be even more so
to Aretha Franklin.

If I were a black male writer, I would think of Frederick Douglass, who
was not just a politician, but as a writer was stunning. In the nineteenth
century I would think of William Wells Brown, Martin Delaney, and cer-

tainly David Walker, who showed not only purpose but method. In the twentieth century I would think of Richard Wright, Jean Toomer, and so on. They mean a great deal to me. I'm black, and they experienced America as blacks. These particular writers may mean more to the black male writer, just as I imagine Jack Johnson would mean a great deal to Jesse Owens, and Jesse Owens a great deal to Arthur Ashe.

CLAUDIA TATE: When you write, are you particularly conscious of preserving certain kinds of images of black people?

ANGELOU: Well, I am some time, though I can't actually say when this happens in the creation of the work. I make writing as much a part of my life as I do eating or listening to music. Once I left church, and as I walked down the street, three young black women stopped me and asked if I would have a glass of wine with them. I said, "Yes." One is a painter; one is an actress; and one a singer. We talked, and when I started to leave, I tried to tell them what it means to me to see young black women. I tried to tell them, but I could hardly explain it. My eyes filled with tears. In one way, it means all the work, all the loneliness and discipline my work exacts, demands, is not in vain. It also means, in a more atavistic, absolutely internal way, that I can never die. It's like living through children. So when I approach a piece of work, *that* is in my approach, whether it's a poem that might appear frivolous or is a serious piece. In my approach I take as fact that my work will be carried on.

TATE: Did you envision young Maya as a symbolic character for every black girl growing up in America?

ANGELOU: Yes, after a while I did. It's a strange condition, being an autobiographer and a poet. I have to be so internal, and yet while writing, I have to be apart from the story so that I don't fall into indulgence. Whenever I speak about the books, I always think in terms of the Maya character. When I wrote the teleplay of *I Know Why the Caged Bird Sings,* I would refer to the Maya character so as not to mean me. It's damned difficult for me to preserve this distancing. But it's very necessary.

TATE: What has been the effect of the women's movement on black women?

ANGELOU: Black women and white women are in strange positions in our separate communities. In the social gatherings of black people, black women have always been predominant. That is to say, in the church it's always Sister Hudson, Sister Thomas, and Sister Witheringay who keep the church alive. In lay gatherings it's always Lottie who cooks, and Mary who's going over to Bonita's, where there is a good party going on. Also, black women are the nurturers of children in our community. White women are in a different position in their social institutions. White men, who are in effect their fathers, husbands, brothers, their sons, nephews, and uncles, say to white women, or imply in any case: "I don't really need you to run my institutions. I need you in certain places and in those places you must be kept—in the bedroom, in the kitchen, in the nursery, and on the pedestal." Black women have never been told this. Black women have not historically stood in the pulpit, but that doesn't undermine the fact that they built the churches and maintain the pulpits. The people who have historically been heads of institutions in black communities have never said to black women—and they too, are their fathers, husbands, brothers, their sons, nephews, and uncles—We don't need you in our institutions." So there is a fundamental difference.

One of the problems I see that faces black women in the eighties, just as it has in the past two decades, has been dealt with quite well in Michele Wallace's *Black Macho and the Myth of the Superwoman. A* number of black men in the sixties fell for a terrible, terrible ploy. They felt that in order to be total and free and independent and powerful, they had to be like white men to their women. So there was a terrible time when black men told their women that if you really love me, you must walk three steps behind me.

I try to live what I consider a "poetic existence." That means I take responsibility for the air I breath and the space I take up. I try to be immediate, to be totally present for all my work. *I try.* This interview with you is a prime example of this. I am withdrawing from the grief that awaits me over the death of someone dear so that I can be present for you, for myself, for your work, and for the people who will read it, so I can tell you exactly how I feel and what I think and try to answer your questions as cheerfully—if I feel cheerful—as I can. That to me is poetic. I try for concentrated consciousness which I miss by more than half, but I'm trying.

TATE: How do you fit writing into your life?

ANGELOU: Writing is a part of my life; cooking is a part of my life. Making love is a part of my life; walking down the street is a part of it. Writing demands more time, but it takes from all of these other activities. They all feed into the writing. I think it's dangerous to concern oneself too damned much with "being an artist." It's more important to get the work done. You don't have to concern yourself with it, just get it done. The pondering pose—the back of the hand glued against the forehead—is baloney. People spend more time posing than getting the work done. The work is all there is. And when it's done, then you can laugh, have a pot of beans, stroke some child's head, or skip down the street.

TATE: What is your responsibility as a writer?

ANGELOU: My responsibility as a writer is to be as good as I can be at my craft. So I study my craft. I don't simply write what I feel, let it all hang out. That's baloney. That's no craft at all. Learning the craft, understanding what language can do, gaining control of the language, enables one to make people weep, make them laugh, even make them go to war. You can do this by learning how to harness the power of the word. So studying my craft is one of my responsibilities. The other is to be as good a human being as I possibly can be so that once I have achieved control of the language, I don't force my weaknesses on a public who might then pick them up and abuse themselves.

During the sixties some lecturers went to universities and took thought-less liberties with young people. They told them "to turn on, tune in, and drop out." People still do that. They go to universities, and students will ask them, "Mr. So-and-So, Ms./Miss/Mrs./Brother/Sister So-and-So, these teachers here at this institution aren't happening, like what should we do?" Many lecturers have said, "Don't take it! Walk out! Let your protest be seen." That lecturer then gets on a plane, first-class, with a double scotch on-the-rocks, jets off to San Juan, Puerto Rico, for a few days' rest, then travels to some other place where he or she is being paid two to three thousand dollars to speak. Those young people risk and sometimes lose their scholastic lives on that zoom because somebody's been irresponsible. I loathe that. I will not do it. I *am* responsible. I *am* trying to be responsible.

So first, I'm always trying to be a better human being, and second, I continue to learn my craft. Then, when I have something positive to say, I can say it beautifully. That's my responsibility.

TATE: Do you see any distinctions in the ways black male and female writers dramatize their themes and select significant events'? This is a general question, but perhaps there is some basis for analysis. Gayl Jones responded to this question by saying she thought women tended to deal with events concerning the family, the community, personal events, that were not generally thought to be important by male writers. She said that male writers tended to select "representative" events for the significant events in their works. Toni Bambara said she thought women writers were concerned with developing a circumscribed place from which the story would unfold. Have you observed such patterns in your reading?

ANGELOU: I find those observations interesting. In fact, the question is very interesting. I think black male writers do deal with the particular, but we are so conditioned by a sexist society that we tend to think when they do so that they mean it representationally; and when black females deal with the particular they only mean it as such. Whether we look at works by Richard Wright, James Baldwin, or John Killens—I'm thinking of novelists—we immediately say this is a generalization; this is meant as an overview, a microcosmic view of the world at large. Yet, if we look at works by Toni Morrison or Toni Bambara, if we look at Alice Walker's work or Hurston's, Rosa Guy's, Louise Meriwether's, or Paule Marshall's, we must say that these works are meant as general statements, universal statements. If *Daddy Was a Numbers Runner* [by Louise Meriwether] is not a microcosm of a macrocosm, I don't know what it is. If Paule Marshall's *Chosen Place and Timeless People* is not a microcosm, I don't know what it is. I don't know what *Ruby* [by Rosa Guy] is if it is not a microcosm of a larger world. I see everybody's work as an example of the particular, which is indicative of the general. I don't see any difference really. Whether it's Claude Brown's or Gayl Jones's. I can look at *Manchild in the Promised Land* and at *Corregidora* and see that these writers are talking about particular situations and yet about the general human condition. They are instructive for the generalities of our lives. Therefore, I won't indulge inherent distinctions between men and women writers.

TATE: Do you consider your quartet to be autobiographical novels or autobiographies?

ANGELOU: They are autobiographies. When I wrote *I Know Why the Caged Bird Sings,* I wasn't thinking so much about my own life or identity. I was thinking about a particular time in which I lived and the influences of that time on a number of people. I kept thinking, what about that time? What were the people around young Maya doing? I used the central figure—myself—as a focus to show how one person can make it through those times.

I really got roped into writing *The Caged Bird.* At that time I was really only concerned with poetry, though I'd written a television series. Anyway, James Baldwin took me to a party at Jules Feiffer's house. It was just the four of us: Jimmy Baldwin and me, Jules Feiffer and his wife, at that time Judy Feiffer. We sat up until three or four o'clock in the morning, drinking scotch and telling tales. The next morning Judy Feiffer called a friend of hers at Random House and said, "You know the poet, Maya Angelou? If you can get her to write a book. . . ." Then Robert Loomis at Random House phoned, and I said, "No, I'm not interested." I went out to

California and produced my series for WNET. Loomis called two or three times, and I said, "No, I'm not interested. Thank you so much." Then, I'm sure he talked to Baldwin because he used a ploy which I'm not proud to say I haven't gained control of yet. He called and said, "Miss Angelou, it's been nice talking to you. I'm rather glad you decided not to write an autobiography because to write an autobiography as literature is the most difficult thing anyone could do." I said, "I'll do it." Now that's an area I don't have control of yet at this age. The minute someone says I can't, all my energy goes up and I say, what? What? I'm still unable to say that you may be wrong and walk away. I'm not pleased with that. I want to get beyond that.

TATE: How did you select the events to present in the autobiographies?

ANGELOU: Some events stood out in my mind more than others. Some, though, were never recorded because they either were so bad or so painful, that there was no way to write about them honestly and artistically without making them melodramatic. They would have taken the book off its course. All my work, my life, everything is about survival. All my work is meant to say, "You may encounter many defeats, but you must not be defeated." In fact, the encountering may be the very experience which creates the vitality and the power to endure.

TATE: You are a writer, poet, director, composer, lyricist, dancer, singer, journalist, teacher, and lecturer. Can you say what the source of such creative diversity is?

ANGELOU: I don't do the dancing anymore. The rest I try. I believe talent is like electricity. We don't understand electricity. We use it. Electricity makes no judgment. You can plug into it and light up a lamp, keep a heart pump going, light a cathedral, or you can electrocute a person with it. Electricity will do all that. It makes no judgment. I think talent is like that. I believe every person is born with talent. I believe anyone can learn the craft of painting and paint.

I believe all things are possible for a human being, and I don't think there's anything in the world I can't do. Of course, I can't be five foot four because I'm six feet tall. I can't be a man because I'm a woman. The physical gifts are given to me, just like having two arms is a gift. In my creative source, wherever that is, I don't see why I can't sculpt. Why shouldn't I? Human beings sculpt. I'm a human being. I refuse to indulge any manmade differences between myself and another human being. I will not do it. I'm not going to live very long. If I live another fifty years, it's not very long. So I should indulge somebody else's prejudice at their whim and not for my own convenience! Never happen! Not me!

TATE: How do you integrate protest in your work?

ANGELOU: Protest is an inherent part of my work. You can't just not write about protest themes or not sing about them. It's a part of life. If I don't agree with a part of life, then my work has to address it.

I remember in the early fifties I read a book, *Dom Casmurro*. It was written by Machado De Assis, a nineteenth-century Brazilian. I thought it was very good. A month later I thought about the book and went back and reread it. Two months later I read the book again, and six months later I realized the sensation that I had had while reading the book was as if I had walked down to a beach to watch a sunset. I had watched the sunset and turned around, only to find that while I had been standing there the tide had come in over my head. I decided to write like that. I would never get on a soapbox; instead, I would pull in the reader. My work is intended to be slowly absorbed into the system on deeper and deeper levels.

TATE: Would you describe your writing process?

ANGELOU: I usually get up at about 5:30, and I'm ready to have coffee by 6, usually with my husband. He goes off to his work around 6:30, and I go off to mine. I keep a hotel room in which I do my work—a tiny, mean room with just a bed, and sometimes, if I can find it, a face basin. I keep a dictionary, a Bible, a deck of cards and a bottle of sherry in the room. I try to get there around 7, and I work until around 2 in the afternoon. If the work is going badly, I stay until 12:30. If it's going well, I'll stay as long as it's going well. It's lonely, and it's marvelous. I edit while I'm working. When I come home at 2, I read over what I've written that day, and then try to put it out of my mind. I shower, prepare dinner, so that when my husband comes home, I'm not totally absorbed in my work. We have a semblance of a normal life. We have a drink together and have dinner. Maybe after dinner I'll read to him what I've written that day. He doesn't comment. I don't invite comments from anyone but my editor, but hearing it aloud is good. Sometimes I hear the dissonance; then I'll try to straighten it out in the morning. When I've finished the creative work and the editing and have six hundred handwritten pages, I send it to my editor. Then we both begin to work. I've kept the same editor through six books. We have a relationship that's kind of famous among publishers, since oftentimes writers shift from one publisher to another for larger advances. I just stay with my own editor, and we'll be together as long as he and I are alive. He understands my work rhythm, and I understand his. We respect each other, but the nit-picking does come. He'll say, "This bothers me—on page twelve, line three, why do you have a comma there? Do you mean to break the flow?"

TATE: How do you feel about your past works?

ANGELOU: Generally, I forget them. I'm totally free of them. They have their own life. I've done well by them, or I did the best I could, which is all I can say. I'm not cavalier about work anymore than I am about sitting here with you, or cooking a meal, or cleaning my house. I've tried to be totally present, so that when I'm finished with a piece of work, I'm finished. I remember one occasion when we were in New York City at the Waldorf Astoria some years ago. I think I was with my sister friends—Rosa [Guy], Paule [Marshall], and Louise [Meriwether]. We were sitting at a table near the bandstand during some tribute for someone, and I felt people staring at me. Someone was singing, say, stage left, and some people were performing a dance. It was very nice, but I felt people staring; so I turned around, and they were. My sister friends were all smiling. I wondered what was happening. I had been following the performance. Well, it turned out that the singer was doing a piece of mine, and they had choreographed a dance to it. I had forgotten the work altogether. The work, once completed, does not need me. The work I'm working on needs my total concentration. The one that's finished doesn't belong to me anymore. It belongs to itself.

TATE: Would you comment on your title selections?

ANGELOU: As you probably know, the title *I Know Why the Caged Bird Sings* is from [Paul Laurence] Dunbar's "Sympathy." *Gather Together in My Name*, though it does have a Biblical origin, comes from the fact I saw so many adults lying to so many young people, lying in their teeth, saying. "You know, when I was young, I never would have done. . . . Why I couldn't. . . . I shouldn't. . . ." Lying. Young people know when you're lying; so I thought for all those parents and nonparents alike who have lied about their past, I will tell it.

    Singin' and Swingin' and Gettin' Merry Like Christmas comes from a time in the twenties and thirties when black people used to have rent parties. On Saturday night from around nine when they'd give these parties, through the next morning when they would go to church and have the Sunday meal, until early Sunday evening was the time when everyone was encouraged to sing and swing and get merry like Christmas so one would have some fuel with which to live the rest of the week.

Just Give Me a Cool Drink of Water 'fore I Diiie refers to my belief that we as individuals in a species are still so innocent that we think we could ask our murderer just before he puts the final wrench upon the throat, "Would you please give me a cool drink of water?" he would do so. That's innocence. It's lovely.

The tune of *Oh, Pray My Wings Are Gonna Fit Me Well* originally comes from a slave holler, and the words from a nineteenth-century spiritual:

> *Oh, pray my wings are gonna fit me well.*
> *I'm a lay down this heavy load.*
> *I tried them on at the gates of hell.*
> *I'm a lay down this heavy load.*

I planned to put all the things bothering me—my heavy load—in that book, and let them pass.

The title poem of *And Still I Rise* refers to the indomitable spirit of black people. Here's a bit of it:

> *You may write me down in history*
> *With your bitter, twisted lies,*
> *You may trod me in the very dirt*
> *But still, like dust, I'll rise.*

TATE: Can black women writers help clarify or help to resolve the black sexist debate that was rekindled by Ntozake Shange's *For Colored Girls Who Have Considered Suicide When the Rainbow Is Enuf* and Michele Wallace's *Black Macho and the Myth of the Superwoman?*

ANGELOU: Neither Miss Shange nor Miss Wallace started the dialogue, so I wouldn't suggest any black woman is going to stop it. If anything could have clarified the dialogue, Toni Morrison's *The Song of Solomon* should have been the work to do that. I don't know if that is a chore or a goal black women writers should assume. If someone feels so inclined, then she should go on and do it.

Everything good tends to clarify. By good I mean well written and well researched. There is nothing so strong as an idea whose time has come. The writer—male or female—who is meant to clarify this issue will do so. I, myself, have no encouragement in that direction. There's a lot that hasn't been said. It may be necessary to hear the male view of *For Colored Girls* in a book or spoken upon the stage. It may be necessary, and I know it will be very painful.

TATE: What writers have influenced your work?

ANGELOU: There were two men who probably formed my writing ambition more than any others. They were Paul Laurence Dunbar and William Shakespeare. I love them. I love the rhythm and sweetness of Dunbar's dialect verse. I love "Candle Lighting Time" and "Little Brown Baby." I also love James Weldon Johnson's "Creation."

I am also impressed by living writers. I'm impressed with James Baldwin. I continue to see not only his craftsmanship but his courage. That means a lot to me. Courage may be the most important of all the virtues because without it one cannot practice any other virtue with consistency. I'm impressed by Toni Morrison a great deal. I long for her new works. I'm impressed by the growth of Rosa Guy. I'm impressed by Ann Petry. I'm impressed by the work of Joan Didion. Her first collection, *Slouching Toward Jerusalem*, contains short pieces, which are absolutely stunning. I would walk fifty blocks in high heels to buy the works of any of these writers. I'm a country girl, so that means a lot.

TATE: Have any of your works been misunderstood?

ANGELOU: A number of people have asked me why I wrote about the rape in *I Know Why the Caged Bird Sings.* They wanted to know why I had to tell that rape happens in the black community. I wanted people to see that the man was not totally an ogre. The hard thing about writing or directing or producing is to make sure one doesn't make the negative person totally negative. I try to tell the truth and preserve it in all artistic forms.

Selected Bibliography

Book Reviews

American Libraries I dl (1970): 714.

Biography: An Interdisciplinary Quarterly 15 (Summer 1992): 243.

Black American Literature Forum 24 (Summer 1990): 221.

———— 24 (Summer 1990): 257.

Black Scholar 12 (Mar. 1981): 87.

Booklist 66 (June 15, 1970): 1256.

———— 66 (July 15, 1970): 1399.

———— 67 (Apr. 1, 1971): 653.

———— 80 (Oct. 15, 1983): 351.

———— 82 (July 1, 1986): 678.

———— 88 (Feb. 15, 1992): 1100.

———— 89 (June 1, 1993): 1864.

———— 91 (Oct. 15, 1994): 412.

Choice 21 (Mar. 1984): 936.

College Literature 22 (Oct. 1995): 91.

English Journal 80 (Dec. 1991): 26.

Guardian Weekly 130 (Feb. 5, 1984): 21.

Harvard Educational Review 40 (Nov. 1970): 681.

Kirkus Review 37 (Dec. 15, 1969): 1292.

———— 37 (Dec. 15, 1969): 1330.

Library Journal 95 (Mar. 15, 1970): 1018.

———— 95 (June 15, 1970): 2320.

———— 95 (Dec. 15, 1970): 4327.

———— 121 (Oct. 15, 1996): 94.

Life. June 5, 1970. 12.

New Statesman. Jan. 27, 1984. 26.

Newsweek. Mar. 2, 1970. 89.

New York Times. Feb. 25, 1970. 45.

Observer (London). Apr. 1, 1984. 22.

————. May 19, 1991. 59.

Publishers Weekly. Dec. 29, 1969. 64.

————. Jan. 25, 1971. 263.

Saturday Review. May 9, 1970. 70.

School Library Journal 30 (Jan. 1984): 42.

———— 35 (Oct. 1988): 39.

———— 39 (Feb. 1993): 33.

Times Educational Supplement. Oct. 19, 1984. 48.

————. Oct. 6, 1989. 38.

Top of the News. Nov. 1970. 92.

————. Apr. 1971. 307.

Wall Street Journal. Apr. 16, 1970. 16.

————. Dec. 8, 1970. 22.

World & I 10 (June 1995): 413.

Books and Articles

Arensberg, Liliane K. "Death as Metaphor of Self in *I Know Why the Caged Bird Sings.*" *College Language Association Journal* 20 (1976): 273–91.

Bertolino, James. "Maya Angelou Is Three Writers: *I Know Why the Caged Bird Sings.*" In *Censored Books: Critical Viewpoints.* Ed. Nicholas Karolides, Lee Burress, and John M. Kean. Metuchen, N.J.: Scarecrow, 1993.

Buss, Helen M. "Reading for the Doubled Discourse of American Women's Autobiography." *Auto-Biography Studies,* 6, no. 1 (Spring 1991): 95–108.

Challener, Daniel Delo. "The Autobiographies of Resilient Children: *Brothers and Keepers, Hunger of Memory, I Know Why the Caged Bird Sings, This Boy's Life,* and *The Woman Warrior.* Ph.D. diss. Brown University, 1993.

Cordell, Shirley J. "The Black Woman: A Focus on 'Strength of Character' in *I Know Why the Caged Bird Sings.*" *Virginia English Bulletin* 36, no. 2 (Winter 1986): 36–39.

Cudjoe, Selwyn R. "Maya Angelou and the Autobiographical Statement." In *Black Women Writers (1950–1980): A Critical Evaluation.* Ed. Mari Evans. Garden City, N.Y.: Anchor-Doubleday, 1984.

Demetrakopoulos, Stephanie A. "The Metaphysics of Matrilinearism in Women's Autobiography: Studies of Mead's *Blackberry Winter,* Hellman's *Pentimento,* Angelou's *I Know Why the Caged Bird Sings,* and Kingston's *The Woman Warrior.*" In *Women's Autobiography: Essays in Criticism.* Ed. Estelle C. Jelinek. Bloomington: Indiana University Press, 1980.

Estes-Hicks, Onita. "The Way We Were: Precious Memories of the Black Segregated South." *African-American Review* 27, no. 1 (Spring 1993): 9–18.

Foster, Francis Smith. "Parents and Children in Autobiography by Southern Afro-American Writers." In *Home Ground: Southern Autobiography.* Ed. J. Bill Berry. Columbia: University of Missouri Press, 1991.

Froula, Christine. "The Daughter's Seduction: Sexual Violence and Literary History." *Signs: Journal of Women in Culture and Society* 11, no. 4 (Summer 1986): 621–44.

Gilbert, Susan. "Maya Angelou's *I Know Why the Caged Bird Sings*: Paths to Escape." *Mount Olive Review* 1, no. 1 (Spring 1987): 39–50.

Graham, Joyce L. "Freeing Maya Angelou's 'Caged Bird.'" Ph.D. diss. Virginia Polytechnic Institute and State University, 1991.

Hagan, Lyman B. *Heart of a Woman, Mind of a Writer, and Soul of a Poet.* Lanham, Md.:
University Press of America, 1997.

Hiers, John T. "Fatalism in Maya Angelou's *I Know Why the Caged Bird Sings.*" *Notes on
Contemporary Literature* 6, no. 1 (1976): 5–7.

Kent, George E. "Maya Angelou's *I Know Why the Caged Bird Sings* and Black Autobiographical Tradition." In *African American Autobiography: A Collection of Critical Essays.* Ed. William L. Andrews. Englewood Cliffs, N.J.: Prentice Hall, 1993.

Kinnamon, Keneth. "Call and Response: Intertextuality in Two Autobiographical
Works by Richard Wright and Maya Angelou." In *Belief vs. Theory in Black Ameri-
can Literary Criticism.* Ed. Joe Weixlmann and Chester Fontenot. Greenwood,
Fla: Penkevill, 1986.

MacKethan, Lucinda H. "Mother Wit: Humor in Afro-American Women's Autobiography." *Studies in American Humor* 4, nos. 1–2 (Spring–Summer 1985): 51–61.

McPherson, Dolly A. "Defining the Self through Place and Culture: Maya Angelou's *I Know Why the Caged Bird Sings.*" *MAWA Review* 5, no. 1 (June 1990): 12–14.

McPherson, Dolly A. *Order Out of Chaos: The Autobiographical Works of Maya Angelou.* London: Virago Press, 1991.

McMurry, Myra K. "Role Playing as Art in Maya Angelou's *Caged Bird.*" *South Atlantic
Bulletin* 41, no. 2 (1976): 106–11.

Megna-Wallace, Joanne. "Simone de Beauvoir and Maya Angelou: Birds of a
Feather." *Simone de Beauvoir Studies* 6 (1989): 49–55.

Moore, Opal. "Learning to Live: When the Bird Breaks from the Cage." In *Censored
Books: Critical Viewpoints.* Ed. Nicholas Karolides, Lee Burress, and John M. Kean.
Metuchen, N.J.: Scarecrow, 1993.

O'Neale, Sondra. "Reconstruction of the Composite Self: New Images of Black
Women in Maya Angelou's Continuing Autobiography." In *Black Women Writers
(1950–1980): A Critical Evaluation.* Ed. Mari Evans. Garden City, N.Y.: Anchor-
Doubleday, 1984.

Premo, Cassie. "When the Difference Becomes Too Great: Images of the Self and
Survival in a Postmodern World." *Genre* 16 (1995): 183–91.

Raynaud, Claudine. "Rites of Coherence: Autobiographical Writings by Hurston,
Brooks, Angelou, and Lorde." Ph.D. diss. University of Michigan, 1991.

Smith, Sidonie Ann. "The Song of a Caged Bird: Maya Angelou's Quest after Self-
Acceptance." *Southern Humanities Review* 7 (Fall 1973): 365–75.

Stepto, R. B. "The *Phenomenal Woman* and the Severed Daughter." *Parnassus* 8, no. 1
(1980): 312–20.

Tawake, Sandra Kiser. "Multi-Ethnic Literature in the Classroom: Whose Standards?" *World Englishes: Journal of English as an International and Intranational Language* 10, no. 3 (Winter 1991): 335–40.

Vermillion, Mary. "Reembodying the Self: Representations of Rape in *Incidents in the Life of a Slave Girl* and *I Know Why the Caged Bird Sings.*" *Biography: An Interdisciplinary Quarterly* 15, no. 3 (Summer 1992): 243–60.

Walker, Pierre A. "Racial Protest, Identity, Words, and Form in Maya Angelou's *I Know Why the Caged Bird Sings.*" *College Literature* 22, no. 3 (Oct. 1995): 91–108.